W9-ATS-780

WITHDRAWN

the Weekend Crafter®

Crochet

Mount Laurel Library
100 Walt Whitman Avenue
Mt. Laurel, NJ 08054-9539
856-234-7319

the Weekend Crafter®

Crochet

20 Simple and Stylish Designs to Wear

JANE DAVIS

LARK BOOKS
A Division of Sterling Publishing Co., Inc.
New York

EDITOR:
MARTHE LE VAN

ART DIRECTOR:
CHARLIE COVINGTON

PHOTOGRAPHY:
EVAN BRACKEN

PHOTOGRAPHY STYLIST:
KATHLEEN HOLMES

ILLUSTRATIONS:
JANE DAVIS

PROOFREADER:
KIM CATANZARITE

EDITORIAL ASSISTANCE:
VERONIKA ALICE GUNTER
RAIN NEWCOMB

Library of Congress Cataloging-in-Publication Data
Davis, Jane, 1959-
Crochet : 20 simple and stylish designs to wear / by Jane Davis.
p. cm. -- (The weekend crafter)
Includes index.
ISBN 1-57990-233-2 (pbk.)
1. Crocheting--Patterns. 2. Vests. 3. Dress accessories. I. Title. II. Series.

TT825.D38 2001
746.43'4032—dc21

2001029380

10 9 8 7 6 5 4 3

Published by Lark Books, a division of
Sterling Publishing Co., Inc.
387 Park Avenue South
New York, N.Y. 10016

© 2001, Jane Davis

Distributed in Canada by Sterling Publishing,
c/o Canadian Manda Group, One Atlantic Ave., Suite 105
Toronto, Ontario, Canada M6K 3E7

Distributed in Australia by Capricorn Link (Australia) Pty Ltd.,
P.O. Box 704, Windsor, NSW 2756 Australia

Distributed in the U.K. by Guild of Master Craftsman Publications Ltd.,
Castle Place 166 High Street, Lewes, East Sussex, England, BN7 1XU.
Tel: (+44) 1273 477374 • Fax: (+44) 1273 478606
Email: pubs@thegmcgroup.com • Web: www.gmcpublications.com

The written instructions, photographs, designs, patterns, and projects in this volume are intended for the personal use of the reader and may be reproduced for that purpose only. Any other use, especially commercial use, is forbidden under law without written permission of the copyright holder.

Every effort has been made to ensure that all the information in this book is accurate. However, due to differing conditions, tools, and individual skills, the publisher cannot be responsible for any injuries, losses, and other damages that may result from the use of the information in this book.

If you have questions or comments about this book, please contact:
Lark Books
67 Broadway
Asheville, North Carolina 28801
(828) 236-9730

Printed in China

All rights reserved

ISBN 1-57990-233-2

CONTENTS

INTRODUCTION

CROCHET MAY BE THE PERFECT CRAFT. It's incredibly fun, simple to learn, and fits effortlessly into your schedule. I've always loved needle arts, and I'm especially drawn to those with wonderful color nuances, and textures of yarn, beads, and threads. I'm also a beader and a knitter, but crochet is something I've done since I was a teenager. I was often more comfortable with crochet than with other needle arts because of its simplicity.

When most people picture crochet they see only vivid patchwork afghans, fringed ponchos, or tea cozies. That's ancient history now. This book looks to the future of crochet apparel by featuring stylish, contemporary designs.

Even if you're a beginner, you'll be able to crochet any of the 20 projects in this book—and look great in them too! Once you grasp a few new terms and see a handful of basic stitches, you'll be off and running, creating project after project of exciting work. From then on, you'll be hooked.

You'll need only a few supplies to start crocheting. A hook, some yarn, scissors, and a tapestry needle are enough to accomplish most patterns. These materials are inexpensive, uncomplicated, and compact. Best of all, they're portable, which is perfect for today's busy, on-the-go lifestyle. Waiting at the doctor's office—why not make a scarf? Commuting to work on the train—how about showing up in a new pair of mittens? What you can make with crochet is limited only by your imagination.

One reason today's fashion crochet is so appealing is that there are simply more and better yarns to choose from. It may not be much of a stretch to picture scarves, hats, and mittens made from crochet. These wonderful winter woollies have always been with us. But the examples in this book rise above the norm by taking advantage of the most modern yarns and using them in innovative combinations and applications. Have you been in a yarn store lately? The selection is almost overwhelming. There are so many colors and textures of yarn that it's difficult not to buy (or at least touch) each and every one. Hand-dyed, or hand-painted wools are artistic just piled up as skeins. Blending mohair, alpaca, wool, and synthetic fibers into various combinations has led to a wider range of products. Crocheters are incorporating slim cords such as cotton tape, embroidery floss, and linen, playing their harder-edged textures off fuzzier yarns for the sake of textural contrast.

My goal in designing these projects was to show that crochet can be innovative while remaining simple. The Enchanted Evening Bag, page 20, and the Tailored Vest, page 49, demonstrate the impact a single stitch pattern can have when crocheted with a spectacular contemporary yarn. There are also patterns with a marked range in stitch variety and construction techniques. The Fern Forest Scarf, page 35, alternates between very tight and very loose stitching again and again to form its length. The Jewel-Tone Scarf, page 24, has a dramatic, scalloped edge, and the Classic Cable Scarf, page 67, has such thick, chunky cables and dense ribbing, you'd swear it was knitted. This is the kind of design innovation and freethinking creativity that continues to propel crochet forward.

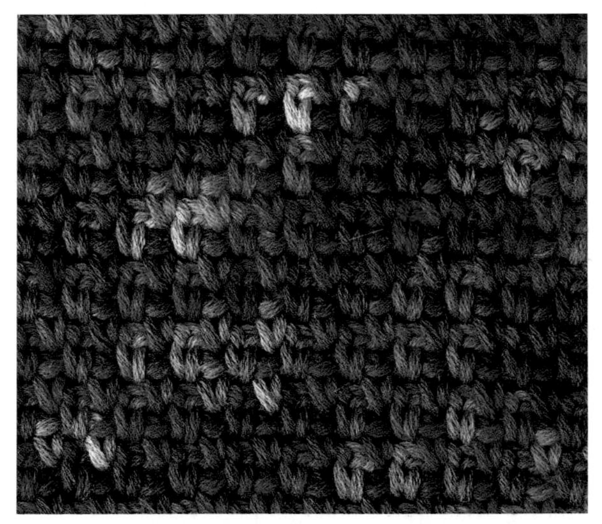

If you're ready to go beyond simple cold weather gear, there are lots of ideas in this book to adorn you from head to toe. Several projects are designed to alter your ordinary store-bought clothes into unique fashion statements. Since you're never completely dressed without the perfect handbag, there are many wonderful crocheted variations offered, from an everyday backpack to an elegant evening bag. Crocheting the fitted projects in this book will sharpen your skills by teaching you sizing and finishing techniques. There's even a terrific pair of Fair Isle Slipper Socks, page 59, to keep your tootsies toasty. As you can see, crochet can take countless shapes and forms when styled as apparel.

You can make any of these projects from start to finish in a single weekend, many in a single day. The designs were selected and arranged with your skill development in mind. Your ability and confidence will grow as you work through the projects from the front to the back of the book. For those of you more visually inclined, I have compiled a pattern library with stitch illustrations to help you along the way. Good luck, and I hope you will have as much fun making these projects as I did!

A NOTE ABOUT CROCHETING

Although crochet has standard stitches and basic patterns, there are variations in the way each needleworker handles the details. The instructions in these pages reflect my way of crocheting, which may be slightly different from the way you or someone you know crochets. You can try it my way, then choose which way you prefer to work.

THE BASICS

This chapter will acquaint you with the essential information unique to crochet. It covers the traits of crochet tools, yarns, and stitches, and includes several useful reference charts.

Tools and Supplies

HOOKS

Hooks come in a variety of materials, from beautiful black walnut to readily available steel and aluminum. The size of the hook is determined by the diameter of its shaft, so the size and shape of the actual hook often vary from company to company. The smallest hook currently available is U.S. size 16 which is .60 mm thick and used for crocheting with thread. The largest is a plastic jumbo hook in size S which is almost ¾ inch (1.9 cm) thick. It's used with several yarns held together as one to crochet.

tip

The goal of crochetwork is to make even and uniform stitches. To accomplish this, it's helpful to use crochet hooks that are the same width all the way to the hook, rather than those that taper down and then widen out just before the hook. Many beginning crocheters often pull their stitches very tight. This makes it difficult to complete each stitch since the loops close tightly around the base of the hook and don't slide easily off the hook. It's then difficult to slide the hook into these tightly formed stitches for the next row.

STITCH MARKERS

Stitch markers vary from plain, plastic loops to sterling silver wire with semiprecious gemstones. In a pinch, however, you can use anything that marks a place in your crochetwork that you can later remove, such as a

Crochet supplies left to right: elastic, yarn, silver stitch markers, scissors, walnut hooks, plastic stitch markers, tapestry needle, beading needle, thread

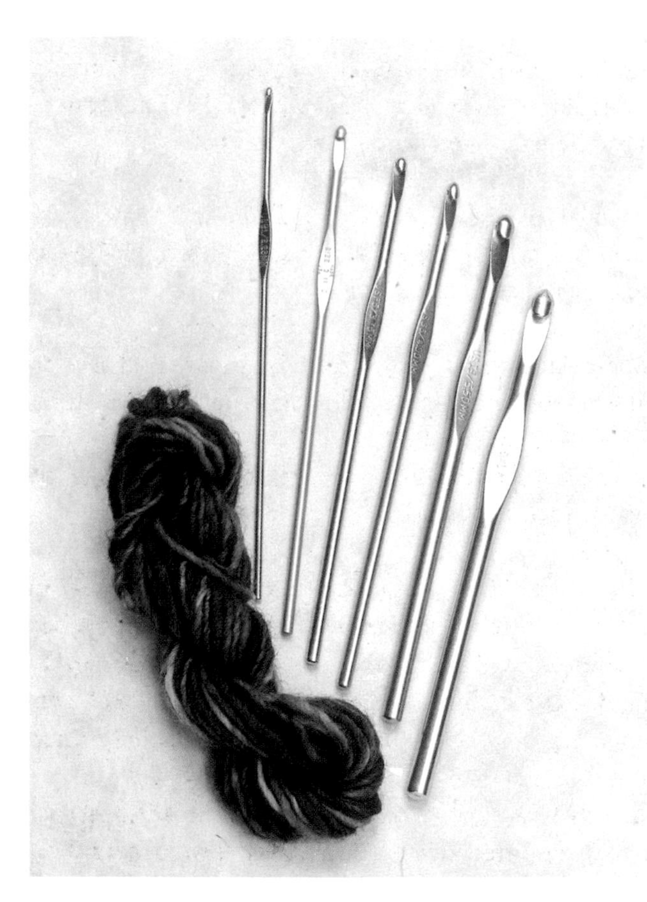

Aluminum, steel and wood crochet hooks in a variety of sizes

contrasting colored yarn or a safety pin. When purchasing stitch markers at a yarn store, be sure to buy the open-ended kind. The ring stitch markers are only for sliding between stitches on knitting needles.

TAPESTRY NEEDLES

Tapestry needles are large, blunt needles that have eyes big enough to thread with yarn. They're available in several sizes and materials. Choose a size that you can easily thread with your yarn.

tip

A simple way to thread a needle with thick fuzzy yarn is to fold the yarn over the needle, then slide the yarn off the needle, and pinch the fold tightly. Next, push the eye of the needle between your pinched fingers, sliding it onto the folded yarn, and pull the yarn through.

Yarn

Today's vast selection of both synthetic and natural fibers has melded into a fascinating array of texture and color that is so much fun to explore. The hardest part is picking one yarn or group of yarns to use.

The easiest yarn to begin with is a basic acrylic or wool with an even, springy texture throughout. Choosing pale colors will help you to double check the accuracy of your stitches, as errors can be more clearly detected in a single light to medium color yarn. Once you are used to crochet, you can use almost any yarn. However, here are a few hints for crocheting with some specialty yarns:

- Try to crochet loosely with chenille or yarns with slubs (thick bumps in the yarn). Working this way, you'll be able to easily slide the hook into all the stitches.

- Many yarns don't have the springy quality of wool or acrylic yarn and are more difficult to handle. If you love a specialty yarn but have trouble crocheting with it, try holding a thin strand of wool, acrylic, or alpaca along with your specialty yarn. You'll find that you can manipulate the stitches much easier. Choosing a contrasting or theme-colored yarn is also a great way to add your own color sense and make your own creation.

YARN SIZES

The following chart lists commonly used terms to describe yarn thickness. It also gives you a general idea of which hook size to use with which yarn. Holding two or more strands of a thin yarn together as one will give you the same result as crocheting with thicker yarn. The texture of the yarn will also make a difference in the gauge of your crochetwork. Don't forget to make a swatch and measure to find your gauge. This will help determine the accurate hook size.

Weight	Description	Hook Sizes
Lace	Threads, very thin yarn	16–1 or B
Fingering	Thin sock yarn, about 1/16 inch (1.6 mm) thick	B–D
Sport	Traditionally used for baby items and thicker socks	E–G
DK	Between sport weight and worsted weight, relatively new in the U.S., though common in the UK	G–H
Worsted	About 1/8 inch (3 mm) thick, there is also a light (towards DK) and heavy (towards Bulky) version. This is the most familiar yarn size and probably the size yarn of most crochet projects made in the U.S. in the last 50 years.	H–I
Bulky	A thick, quick yarn to crochet	I–K
Super Bulky	A very thick yarn, 1/4 inch (6 mm) or more in diameter	K and larger

YARN TYPES AND TEXTURES

There is an amazing variety of yarn textures on the market today. Many things can affect a yarn's texture. The following glossary lists of some of these factors.

Bouclé. A bumpy-textured yarn made by plying two or more strands of yarn together so that they create little loops along the yarn's surface.

Chenille. A soft fuzzy-textured yarn made by plying strands of thread together with many small strands caught perpendicular to the yarn so that they tuft out.

Mercerized. Cotton thread treated with sodium hydroxide which pre-shrinks it, gives it a shiny finish, and allows it to better absorb dye colors.

Mohair. An airy, hairy yarn from the Angora goat. Blends that resemble mohair are called mohair-type yarn.

Ply. The number of strands twisted together to make the finished yarn or thread.

Slub. A thick bump along the yarn made by spinning the yarn more loosely at that point and/or having more fiber at that point. Originally this was not desirable in spinning because it showed the spinner lacked control over the materials. Now it's a design element in many yarns.

Space-dyed. A variegated yarn that has had different colors of dye poured along spaces of the skein of yarn.

Spot-dyed. A variegated yarn that has been treated with spots of dye throughout the skein of yarn.

Variegated. A yarn dyed different colors so that it changes from one color to the next along the length of yarn. This can be done by hand or machine. Machine dying results in a regular repeat of the color pattern while hand dying produces a more random effect.

Techniques

TERMINOLOGY

Many of the basic terms and phrases used in crochet instructions are unique. They regularly appear in abbreviated form. For your convenience, a table of abbreviations appears on page 19.

Brackets [ ] or parentheses ( ). Used to enclose a sequence of stitches meant to be repeated. You'll be instructed how many times to repeat the sequence following the closing punctuation.

Chain space. To create a space by making a chain between stitches. To stitch in a chain space, pass the hook through the loop of the chain space and complete the stitch.

Foundation. The beginning chain of your project.

Place marker. To slide a stitch marker into the two loops of the top chain of the stitch just completed.

Post. The vertical part of the stitch, more evident in double and triple crochet stitches.

Round. A horizontal line of stitches in which the work spirals and there is no step up to the next level. This is found only on round spiraling crochetwork.

Row. A horizontal line of stitches in which a level is completed and there is a step up to the next level. This can be a flat piece worked back and forth or a round piece in which each round is completed before a step up to the next row.

Shell. A group of stitches formed in the same stitch or space.

tip

The turning chain is sometimes used as one of the stitches for the row and sometimes it's just to get you to the right level to begin the next row. This book uses both techniques depending on the project. When the turning chain is used as a stitch on the row, you don't crochet in the first stitch at the beginning of the row (the turning chain takes up this space) and you do crochet in the top chain of the turning chain.

Step up. To chain one or more stitches at the end of a row in order to position the yarn and hook at the level of a new row. For single crochet you chain one, for half double crochet you chain two, for double crochet you chain three. This is also called the **turning chain.** In crochet directions, it is sometimes listed at the end of a row and sometimes at the beginning of the row. All the patterns in this book have the step up at the beginning of the row except the Linen Tank Top, page 55.

Tail. The loose end of the yarn.

Turning chain. Another name for step up.

Weave in end. To pass through the last loop of yarn with a tapestry needle, then stitch the tail into the crochetwork for about 2 inches (5 cm) so it's hidden. Stitch back and forth, locking the yarn in place so it won't loosen. Clip the tail close to the crochetwork.

Work even. To continue in a pattern stitch with no increase or decrease until the piece measures the indicated size, or for the number of rows or stitches indicated.

Yarn over. To wrap the yarn around the hook from back to front.

GAUGE

One of the most common phrases in knitting and crochet books is, "take time to check gauge." Why is that said so much, and what does it mean? Even though the directions for making each crochet stitch are specific, every person is an individual and has her own slightly different way of holding the yarn and the hook and making the stitches. Because of this, even though two people use the same tools and materials, they may make their stitches a different size. Project instructions are based on a specific stitch size. This doesn't matter too much for a scarf, but for something like a vest, if you don't match the gauge given, your finished piece will end up too small or too large. To check your gauge, make a sample with the materials listed, at least 4 inches (10.2 cm) square, then measure the stitches and rows to see if they're the same as the gauge listed. If they're too big, you'll need to make another sample using a smaller hook size. Use a larger hook if your stitches are too small. This does take extra time, but it's the only way you'll end up with the finished project you're expecting.

Basic Stitches

HOLDING THE YARN AND HOOK

To make even stitches, you'll need to be able to control the tension of the yarn and hold your project as you work. A good way to control the tension is to wrap the yarn around the little finger of your left hand, then pass it behind and over your index finger. This way the yarn isn't too tight or loose as you wrap the hook and pull through loops for each stitch. Use your thumb and other fingers on your left hand to hold the work as you make your stitches.

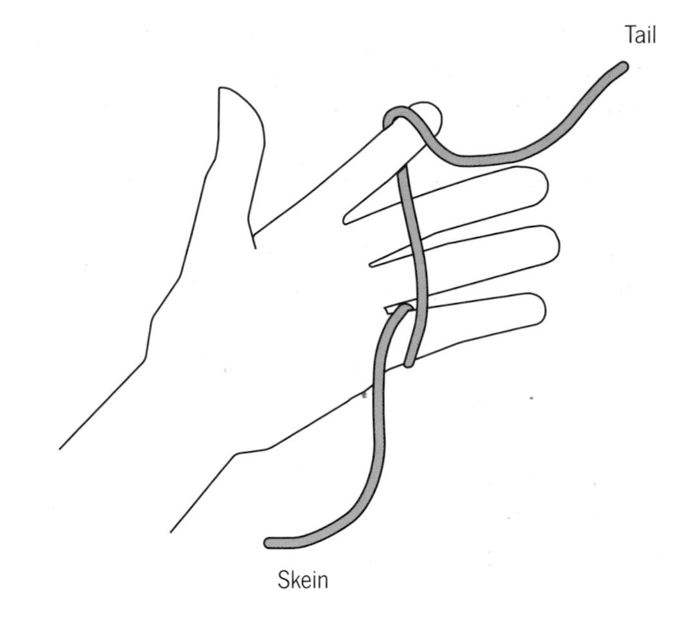

MAKING A SLIP KNOT

A slip knot is the first step in almost all crochet projects.

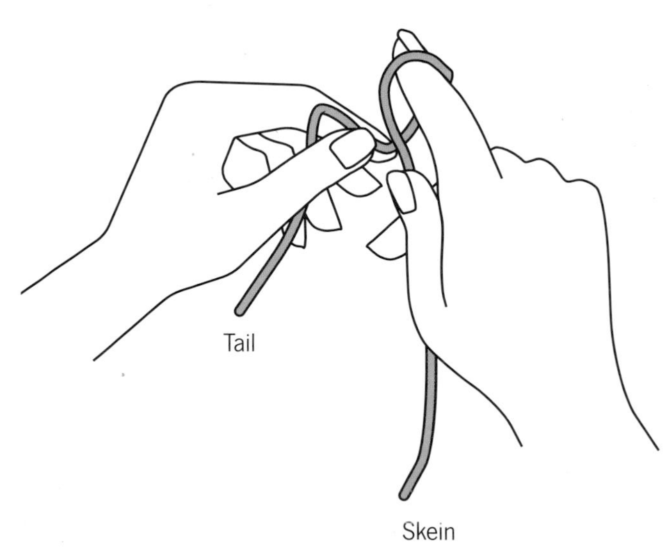

To make a slip knot:

1 Hold the tail of the yarn in your right hand and loop the yarn over itself with the skein-end in your left hand.

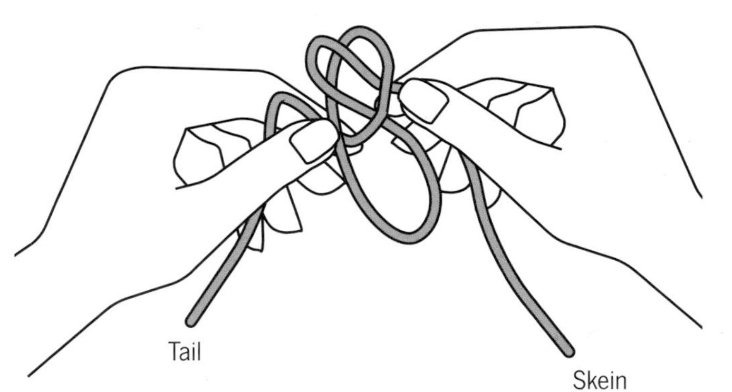

2 With your left hand, push a second loop up through the bottom of the first loop.

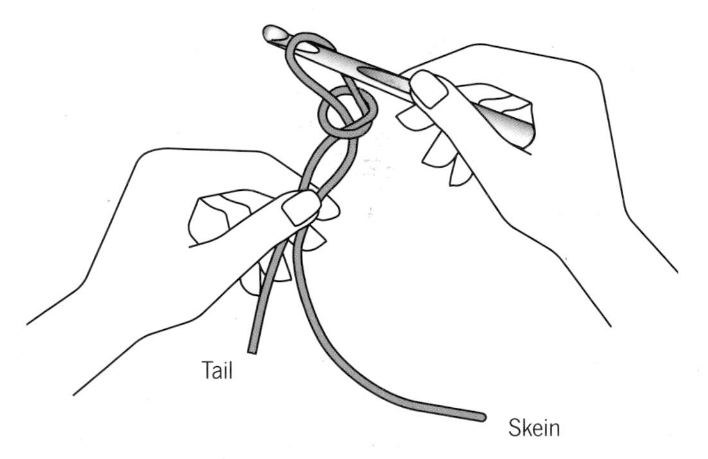

3 Put your hook through the new loop. Tighten the knot by pulling on both ends of the yarn, then pull on the skein end of the yarn to make the slip knot tighten up to the hook.

MAKING A CHAIN (ch)

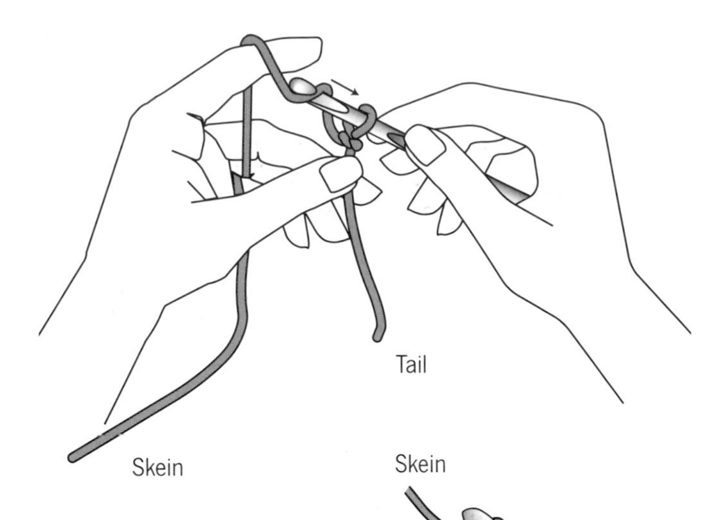

Skein

Tail

Almost every project in this book begins by making a chain of stitches as a foundation for your crochetwork. To make a chain, first make a slip knot. With the hook through the slip knot, wrap the yarn around the hook (yo), and pull it through the slip knot (loop). Repeat this step to make the number of chains indicated in the instructions.

SINGLE CROCHET (sc)

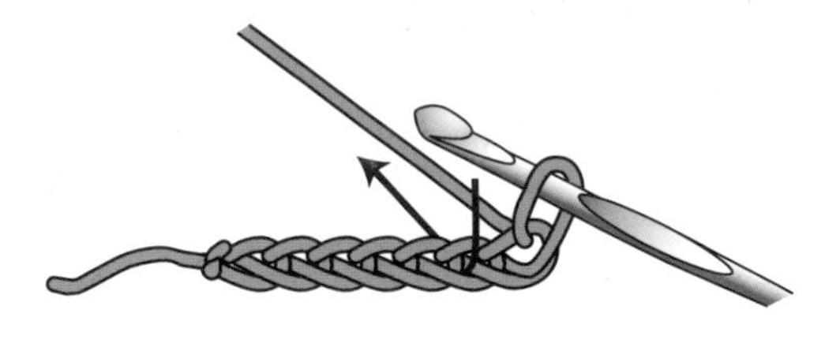

1 Push the hook through the second chain from the hook (1 chain and 1 loop on hook).

2 Wrap the yarn around the hook (yo), and pull through the chain (2 loops on hook).

3 Wrap the yarn around the hook again, and pull through both loops on the hook (1 loop on hook).

SLIP STITCH (sl st)

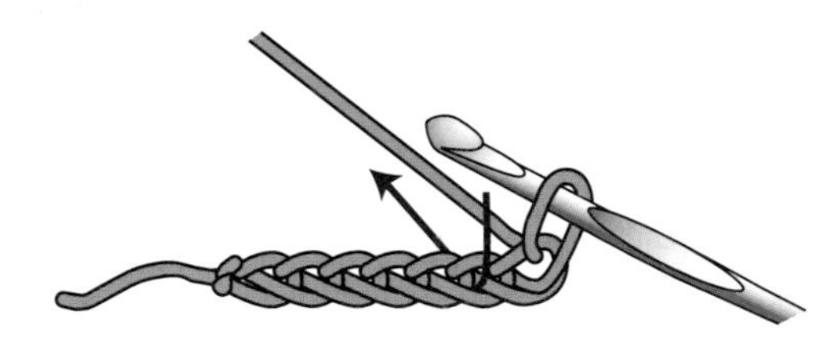

1 Push the hook through the second chain from the hook (1 chain and 1 loop on hook).

2 Wrap the yarn around the hook (yo), and pull through both stitches on the hook (1 loop on hook).

HALF DOUBLE CROCHET (hdc)

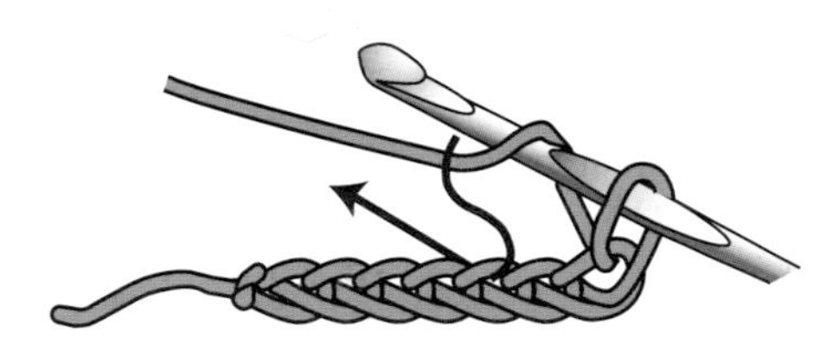

1 Wrap the yarn around the hook, then push the hook through the third chain from the hook (1 chain and 2 loops on hook).

2 Wrap the yarn around the hook (yo), and pull through the chain (3 loops on hook).

3 Wrap the yarn around the hook (yo), and pull through all the loops on the hook (1 loop on hook).

DOUBLE CROCHET (dc)

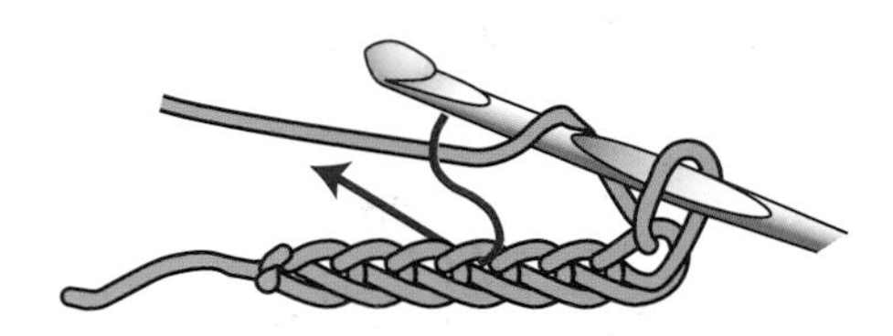

1 Wrap the yarn around the hook, insert the hook through the fourth chain from the hook (1 chain and 2 loops on hook).

2 Wrap the yarn around the hook (yo), and pull through the chain (3 loops on hook).

3 Wrap the yarn around the hook (yo), and pull through 2 loops on the hook (2 loops on hook).

4 Wrap the yarn around the hook (yo), and pull through the last 2 loops on the hook (1 loop on hook).

HALF TRIPLE CROCHET (htr)

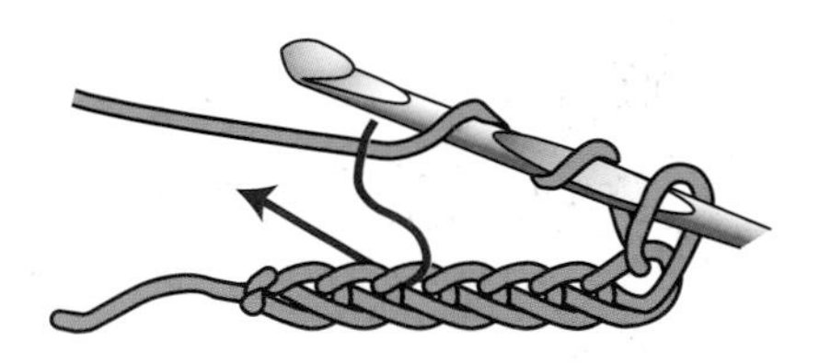

1 Wrap the yarn around the hook (yo) twice, and push the hook through the fifth chain from the hook (1 chain and 3 loops on hook).

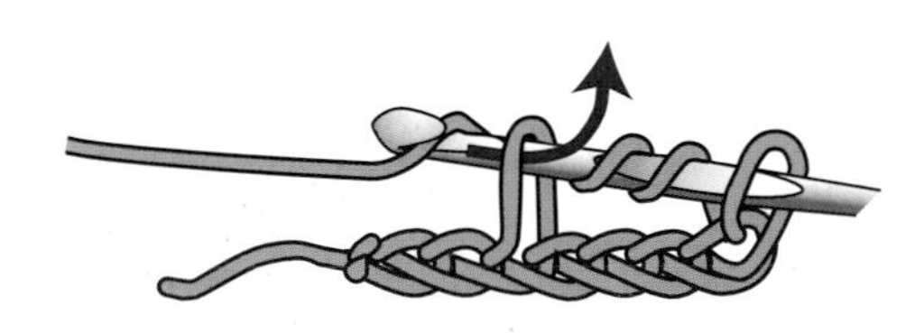

2 Wrap the yarn around the hook (yo), and pull through the chain (4 loops on hook).

3 Wrap the yarn around the hook (yo), and pull through all the loops on the hook (1 loop on hook).

TRIPLE CROCHET (tr)

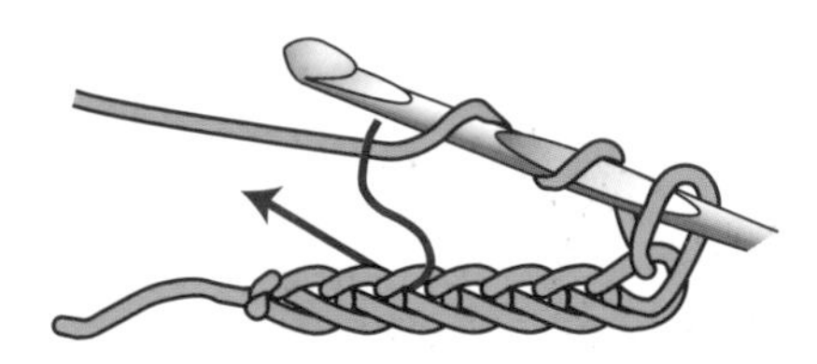

1 Wrap the yarn around the hook (yo) twice, and push the hook through the fifth chain from the hook (1 chain and 3 loops on hook).

2 Wrap the yarn around the hook (yo), and pull through the chain (4 loops on hook).

3 Wrap the yarn around the hook (yo), and pull through 2 loops on the hook (3 loops on hook).

4 Wrap the yarn around the hook (yo), and pull through 2 loops on the hook (2 loops on hook).

5 Wrap the yarn around the hook (yo), and pull through 2 loops on the hook (1 loop on hook).

CROCHETING INTO ROWS OF STITCHES

The preceding instructions show you how to begin a row of crochetwork from the foundation chain. To crochet into the following rows of stitches, push the hook through both sides of the top loop on the edge of the fabric, then complete the stitch as usual.

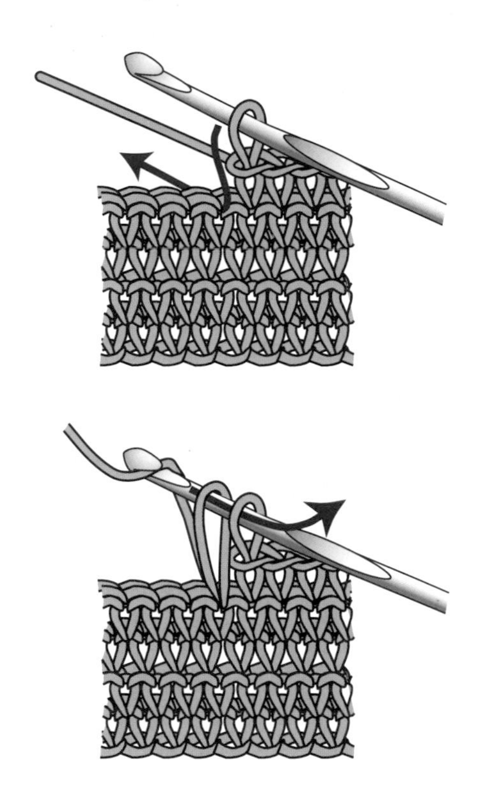

CHAIN SPACE (ch sp)

In patterns such as the seed stitch, you'll make a single crochet (sc), then make one chain (ch 1), then make another single crochet two stitches away ("sc in 2nd st," or "skip next st, sc in next st"). The chain between the two single crochet stitches is called a chain space (ch sp). Sometimes, on a following row, you crochet into this chain space (ch sp). This chain space can be any number of stitches between any kind of stitches.

JOINING INTO A RING

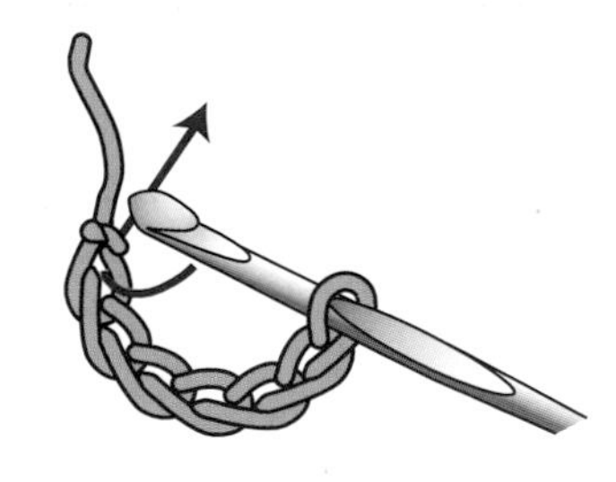

When beginning a circular project, you'll make a chain and join it into a ring with a slip stitch (sl st). To do this, insert the hook into the first chain you made, yarn over (yo), and pull through the chain and the loop on the hook. Pull your work tightly. Your first row or round will be made by inserting the hook into the ring, rather than into the chains of the ring, to make each stitch.

JOINING AT THE END OF A ROUND

At the end of each row on a circular project, such as the body of the Confetti Backpack (page 43), you'll need to complete the row by joining the first and last stitch together with a slip stitch. To do this you'll make a slip stitch in the last chain of the step up chain.

Variations

SINGLE CROCHET INTO THE BACK HALF OF THE STITCH

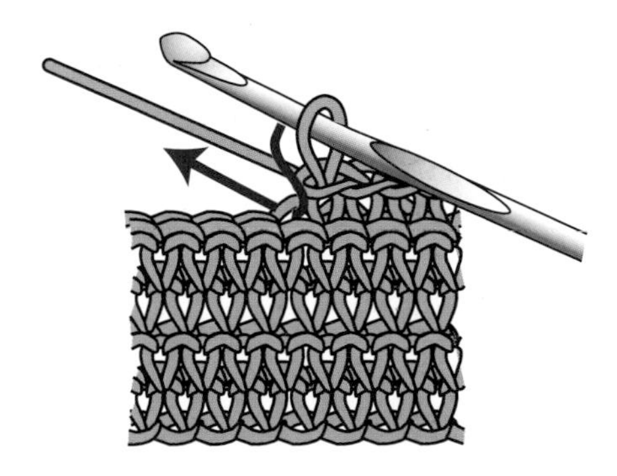

The top surface of each stitch is made of a chain. The back half of the stitch is the single strand of the loop which is farthest away from the side you're working. Push the hook into that strand only, then complete the stitch.

CROCHETING BACKWARDS

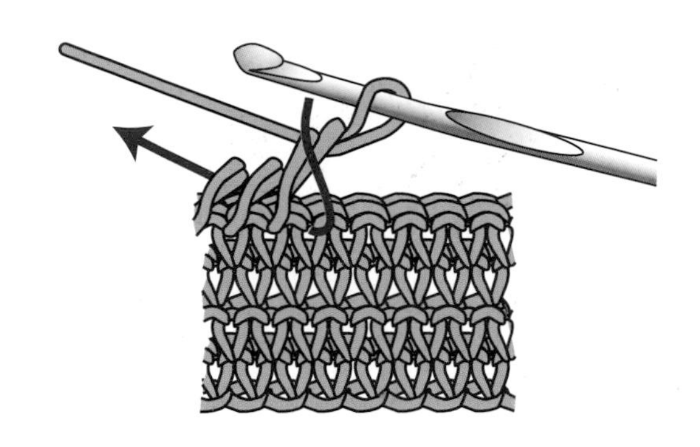

Single crocheting backwards around the edge of a project creates a textured, undulating finished edge. To crochet backwards, insert the hook into the stitch to the right of the beginning of the yarn. Wrap the yarn around the hook and pull through the stitch on the hook. Now, wrap the yarn around the hook and pull through both loops on the hook. Be sure to make very loose stitches so they don't pull on the edges of the piece, causing it to pucker.

MAKING A SHELL

Make the indicated number of stitches in the same place, such as 4 double crochet in 1 stitch, or 4 double crochet in 1 chain space. How many stitches are in one place, and how big the space is (1 stitch or a chain space of 3 stitches) will determine how much the shell fans out or stays as a square block of stitches.

Advanced Stitches

FRONT POST DOUBLE CROCHET (fpdc)

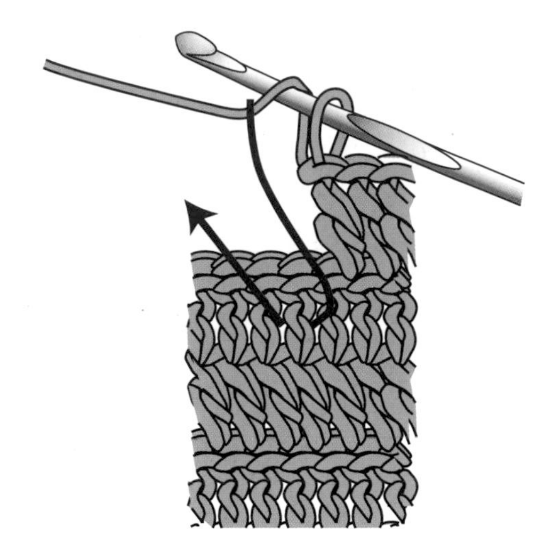

1 Wrap the yarn around the hook, and push the hook behind the post of the stitch in the row below.

2 Complete as in steps 2–4 for double crochet (dc).

BACK POST DOUBLE CROCHET (bpdc)

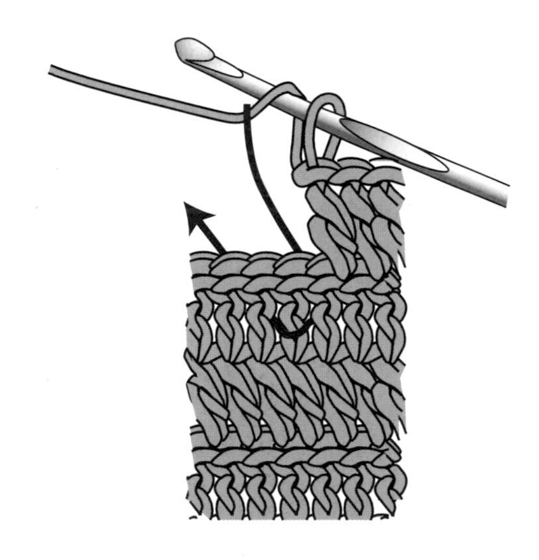

1 Wrap the yarn around the hook. Entering from the back side of the fabric, push the hook around the post of the stitch in the row below.

2 Complete as in steps 2–4 for double crochet (dc).

FRONT POST HALF TRIPLE CROCHET (fphtr)

1 Wrap the yarn around the hook (yo) twice. Push the hook behind the post of the stitch in the row below.

2 Complete as in steps 2 and 3 for half triple crochet (htr).

CHANGING COLORS

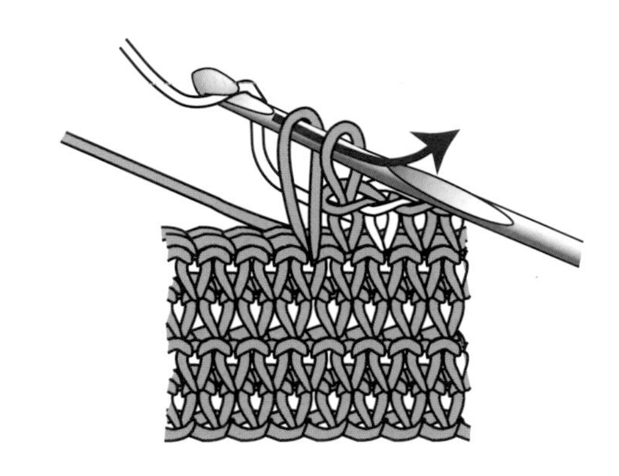

When crocheting with more than one color, it helps to understand what's happening to the stitches as they're made. If you change colors for a single crochet stitch, your new color will slant to the left at the top. The last yarn over (yo) you pull through the last two loops on the hook actually sits between the stitch just made and the next stitch, causing the slant. The next row of stitches passes through this yarn over, breaking up the color pattern and making it look awkward. Because of this, most times you will need to change to the new yarn color for the last yarn over of the stitch ***before*** the stitch with the new color. Doing so will give your colorwork a much smoother appearance. This is how the Fair Isle Slipper Socks, page 59, are crocheted for two rows when changing from blue to red. For the Star Pocket, page 41, and Star Hat, page 46, the colors need to slant both to the right and the left to make the star pattern. These patterns have a mix of pulling the new yarn color through on the last stitch of the old color, or completing the stitch with the old color, and ***then*** changing to the new color.

Abbreviations

beg	begin/beginning
bpdc	back post double crochet
ch	chain
chs	chains
ch sp	chain space
dc	double crochet
fpdc	front post double crochet
fphtr	front post half triple crochet
hdc	half double crochet
hk	hook
htr	half triple crochet
rep	repeat
reps	repeats
rnd	round
sc	single crochet
sl st	slip stitch
st	stitch
sts	stitches
tr	triple crochet
yo	yarn over

Crochet Hook Sizes

Use the following table as a guide for the hook sizes used in this book. Keep in mind that sizes may vary slightly from company to company between letter name and metric size. Begin your project with whichever size hook gives you the intended gauge.

U.S.	Metric	U.K.
D/3	3.25	10
E/4	3.5	9
F/5	3.75	8
G/6	4	7
H/8	5	6
I/9	5.5	5
J/10	6	4
K/10.5	6.5	2

U.S. and European Equivalents

Crochet terminology is different in America than in European countries. All of the instructions in this book are written using American standards. The following table shows the equivalent European terms.

U.S. Terms	European Equivalents
slip stitch (sl st)	single crochet
single crochet (sc)	double crochet
half double crochet (hdc)	half treble crochet
double crochet (dc)	treble crochet
triple crochet (tr)	double treble

Enchanted Evening Bag

Need to accessorize that special evening out? Reach for this lovely little bag and add a touch of elegance wherever you go. A dressy cotton cord and an all-over pebble stitch make this bag exceptionally sleek and refined. Use a shell-button clasp for extra sparkle.

YOU WILL NEED

1 skein worsted weight cotton yarn that will obtain the gauge given below; approximately 1.75 ounces (50 g), or 108 yards (100 m)

1 button, approximately 1 inch (2.54 cm) diameter

Size E hook

Tapestry needle

Steam iron

Scissors

FINISHED MEASUREMENTS

4½ inches (11.4 cm) x 5½ inches (14 cm) with a 36-inch (91.4 cm) strap

GAUGE (in pattern)

5 sts = 1 inch (2.5 cm)

2 rows = 1 inch (2.5 cm)

STITCHES USED

ch

sc

dc

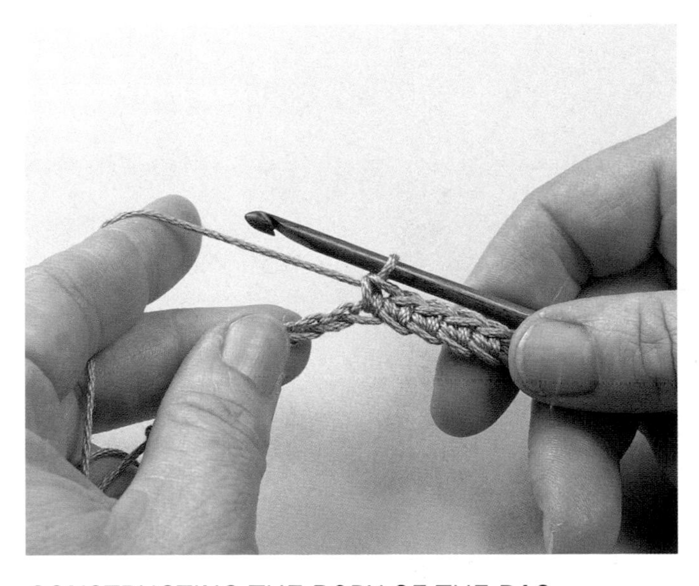

CONSTRUCTING THE BODY OF THE BAG

1 Beg at the top flap: Foundation: Ch 23, turn. Row 1: Ch 1, sc in 2nd ch from hk and each ch across (see photo), turn (23 sts total).

2 Row 2: Ch 3, (skip 2 sts, [dc, ch 1, dc] in next st as in photo) 7 times, turn (22 sts total).
Row 3: Ch 2, [sc, dc] 11 times, turn (22 sts total).
Rep row 3 until fabric is 12 inches (30.5 cm) long. Weave in ends.

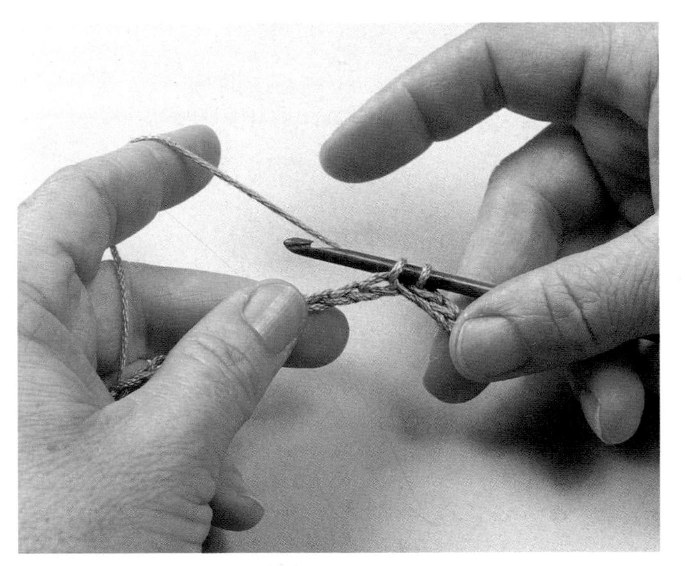

MAKING THE SHOULDER STRAP

3 Ch 160, sl st in back half of each st (see photo).

ASSEMBLING THE BAG

4 Measure 1½ inches (3.8 cm) from the top and fold over the openwork flap. Fold the bottom up 5 inches (12.7 cm). Use an iron to steam-press the folds in place. St the side seams together and st the strap to the fold of the flap (see photo).

5 Make a ch st loop long enough to slip over the button, and sew it in place on the edge of the flap (see photo). Sew the button to the front of the bag.

This project was crocheted with Tahki Imports' Cotton Classic in tea rose #3346 (100% mercerized cotton).

Jewel-Tone Scarf and Hat

Add elegance to your wardrobe with this sophisticated scarf and hat set. Its pattern was inspired by a technique used chiefly for afghans known as "mile-a-minute." Here, the crochet bands vary in size and color to create a truly original fashion statement.

Scarf

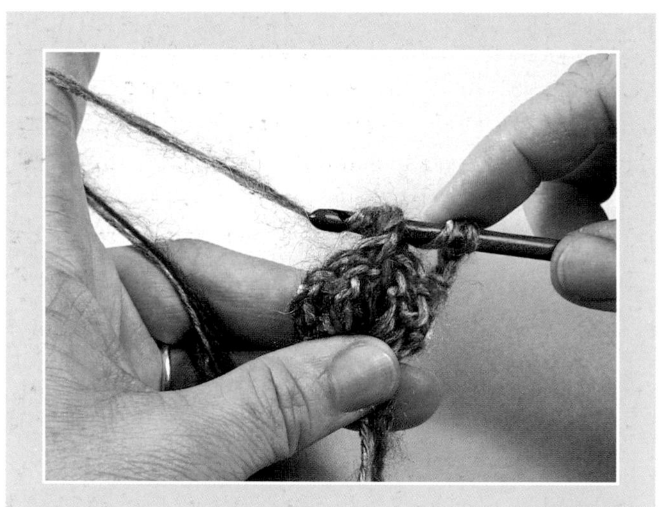

BASIC 2-SHELL PATTERN

Foundation: Ch 5, join into a ring with a sl st.
Row 1: Ch 3, 2 dc in ring, ch 3, 3 dc in ring, turn (1 2-shell section complete).
Row 2: Ch 3, 3 dc in ch sp (see photo), ch 3, 3 dc in same ch sp, 1 dc into 3rd ch of ch 3 at beg of row 1, turn (2 2-shell sections complete).
Row 3: Ch 3, 3 dc in ch sp, ch 3, 3 dc in same ch sp, 1 dc in next ch sp, turn (3 2-shell sections complete).

YOU WILL NEED

Yarn A: 1 skein worsted weight mohair-type yarn that will obtain the gauge given below; approximately 2 ounces (56.5 g), or 179.35 yards (165 m)

Yarn B: 1 skein sport weight yarn; approximately 2 ounces (50 g), or 105 yards (110 m)

Yarn C: 3 skeins worsted weight chenille yarn; approximately 1.4 ounces (39.2 g), or 95 yards (85.5 m) per skein

Yarn D: 1 skein sport weight yarn; approximately 2 ounces (50 g), or 120 yards (110 m)

Yarn E: 1 skein sport weight yarn; approximately 1.75 ounces (50 g), or 178 yards (163 m)

Yarn F: 1 skein worsted weight bouclé yarn; approximately 3 ounces (85 g), or 182 yards (166 m)

Size H hook

Size G hook

Tapestry needle

Scissors

FINISHED MEASUREMENTS

8 inches (20.3 cm) x 56 inches (142.2 cm)

GAUGE (of 2-shell repeats with size H hk using Yarn A and Yarn B held together as 1)

2 shells = 2 inches (5 cm)

5 rows = 4 inches (10.2 cm)

STITCHES USED

ch

sl st

sc

dc

tip

This is a great project for using up leftover skeins. Try combining many different textures and colors to create a new look. Always use a bouclé for joining because it makes a nice texture without showing individual stitches.

CREATING THE CENTER STRIP

1 Hold Yarn A and Yarn B together as 1 yarn. Use the size H hk to make 1 strip of 66 2-shell sections. Weave in ends. Hold Yarn D and Yarn E together as 1 yarn. Attach them to a ch sp along the strip (see photo). Ch 3, make 2 dc in the same space, then make 3 dc in each space along the edges of the strip, making 8 dc in the space at each end. Join the beg and end with a sl st. Weave in ends. Hold Yarn D and Yarn F together as 1 yarn. Attach them to a st along the strip. Ch 3, make 1 dc in the next st [ch 1, 1 dc in the next 2 sts] rep around, making 2 dc in each of the 8 sts at each end of the strip. Join to the 3rd ch with a sl st. Weave in end.

FASHIONING THE SIDE STRIPS

2 Use Yarn E and the size G hk to make 2 separate strips of 100 2-shell sections each. Weave in ends.

Attach Yarn C to a ch sp along 1 of the strips. Make 3 dc in each ch sp and 2 dc in each dc sp along the edges of the strip (see photo), making 8 dc in the space at each end. Join the beg and end with a sl st. Weave in ends. Rep step 3 to make a 2nd strip.

JOINING

3 Lay the center strip and 1 side strip on a flat surface. Line them up next to each other so the larger strip extends beyond the smaller strip equally at both ends. Using Yarn F and the size H hk, sc through the edges of both strips, joining them together (see photo). Every so often, double-check that the strips are still lining up properly by laying them flat and making sure the large strip will extend the same distance at each end. Adjust, if necessary, by skipping a st on the strip that is getting too long. Rep for the other side of the large strip and the 2nd small strip. Weave in ends.

This project was crocheted with Lion Brand's Imagine "Blue on Blue" (Yarn A, 80% acrylic and 20% mohair); Mondial's Raffia Jeans in light blue multi (Yarn B, 60% cotton, 20% acrylic, and 20% viscose); Lion Brand's Chenille Sensations "London Print" (Yarn C, 100% acrylic); Blue Sky Alpacas' Purple #53 (Yarn D, 100% alpaca); Patons' Astra in Turquoise #2945 (100% acrylic); and Patons' Canadian Bouclé #7075 (97% acrylic and 3% nylon).

Hat

YOU WILL NEED

Yarn A: 1 skein worsted weight mohair-type yarn that will obtain the gauge given below; approximately 2 ounces (56.5 g), or 179.35 yards (165 m)

Yarn B: 1 skein sport weight yarn; approximately 2 ounces (50 g), or 105 yards (110 m)

Yarn C: 3 skeins worsted weight chenille yarn; approximately 1.4 ounces (39.2 g), or 95 yards (85.5 m) per skein

Yarn D: 1 skein sport weight yarn; approximately 2 ounces (50 g), or 120 yards (110 m)

Yarn E: 1 skein sport weight yarn; approximately 1.75 ounces (50 g), or 178 yards (163 m)

Yarn F: 1 skein worsted weight bouclé yarn; approximately 3 ounces (85 g), or 182 yards (166 m)

Size H hook

Size G hook

Tapestry needle

Scissors

FINISHED MEASUREMENTS

23 inches (58.4 cm) circumference

GAUGE (of 2-shell reps using size H hk and Yarn A and Yarn B held together as 1)

2 shells = 2 inches (5 cm)

5 rows = 4 inches (10.2 cm)

STITCHES USED

ch

ch sp

sl st

sc

dc

tr

BEGINNING WITH A TUBE

1 Hold Yarn A and Yarn B together as 1 yarn. Use the size H hk to make a strip of 25 2-shell sections, joining into a circle on the last 2-shell section. To join into a circle, make the 1st 3 dc in the ch sp, then slide the hk through the beg ring of the strip and make a ch, encasing the ring in the st (see photo).
Finish the 2-shell section by making 3 dc in the same ch sp and 1 dc in the next ch sp. Weave in ends. You now have a tube.

CROCHETING THE HAT

2 Row 1: Holding Yarn C and Yarn E together as 1 yarn, join to 1 of the ch sp on 1 side of the tube. This will be the top half of the hat. Ch 3, 2 dc in ch sp, then make 3 dc in each ch sp and dc around the strip. Join together with a sl st. Weave in ends.
Row 2: Holding Yarn D and Yarn F together as 1 yarn, ch 3, 1 dc in every other st around the hat (see photo) to the last 2 sts. Join with a sl st to the 3rd ch.

3 Row 3: Ch 4, 1 tr in every other ch sp around the hat (see photo). Join with a sl st to the 4th ch.
Row 4: Change to Yarn A and Yarn B. Ch 3, 1 dc in each ch sp around. Join with a sl st to 3rd ch. Weave through top of last row to close hole. Weave in ends.

CREATING THE BRIM

4 Row 1: Attach Yarn C and Yarn E to the bottom edge of the hat, ch 3, 2 dc in 1st ch sp, then 3 dc in each ch sp and dc along the bottom of the hat. Make 5 rows of sc in each st. Change to Yarn D and Yarn F and make 2 rows of sc in each st. Change to size G hk and make 2 more rows of sc in each st. Weave in ends. Fold brim up about 1¼ inches (3.2 cm).

This project was crocheted with Lion Brand's Imagine "Blue on Blue" (Yarn A, 80% acrylic and 20% mohair); Mondial's Raffia Jeans in light blue multi (Yarn B, 60% cotton, 20% acrylic, and 20% viscose); Lion Brand's Chenille Sensations "London Print" (Yarn C, 100% acrylic); Blue Sky Alpacas' Purple #53 (Yarn D, 100% alpaca); Patons' Astra in Turquoise #2945 (100% acrylic); and Patons' Canadian Bouclé #7075 (97% acrylic and 3% nylon).

Autumn Leaves Appliqué

Small crochet shapes make pretty decorations on all kinds of store-bought items. This quick leaf appliqué and edging can be stitched on everything from a vest to hand towels, blankets, or carryalls. It's easy to vary the number of leaves on the stem or the length of the edging once you learn the stitch pattern.

YOU WILL NEED

1 skein heavy worsted weight yarn that will obtain the gauge given below; approximately 3.5 ounces (100 g)

Size G hook

Sewing needle

Sewing thread

Steam iron

Purchased vest

Scissors

FINISHED MEASUREMENTS

Leaf: 1½ inches (3.8 cm)

Edging: ¾ inch (1.9 cm) wide

GAUGE (in edging)

2 reps = 1¼ inches (3.2 cm)

STITCHES USED

ch

sl st

sc

hdc

dc

htr

tr

tip

This basic leaf pattern inspires a lot of creativity. You can make leaves of different sizes by increasing or decreasing the number of stitches in each leaf. Your leaves can also tilt to one side or another simply by adding or deleting one or two stitches on one side of the leaf or the other.

FORMING THE BASIC LEAF

1 Ch 4, join into a ring with a sl st. Ch 2, 1 hdc in ring, 2 dc in ring, 1 htr in ring, 2 tr in ring, ch 3 (see photo).

2 2 tr in ring, 1 htr in ring, 2 dc in ring, 1 hdc in ring, ch 2, sl st in ring (see photo), pull tight.

MAKING MORE THAN ONE LEAF ON A SPRIG

3 Ch 3 between leaves, form a new leaf (see photo), making 2 or 3 total. Sl st in the base of the 1st leaf, and make a ch for the stem. Weave in the end, or, for a sturdier stem, sl st back up the ch to the leaves before weaving in the end.

ATTACHING THE LEAVES

4 Pin the sprigs in place where you want them on the vest. Sew them down around their edges with the needle and thread.

CALCULATING THE LENGTH OF THE EDGING

5 Measure around the bottom edge and collar of the vest and add the measurements together. Double the number and ch that many sts plus 10, turn.

This project was crocheted with Manos del Uruguay in rhubarb #109 (100% wool).

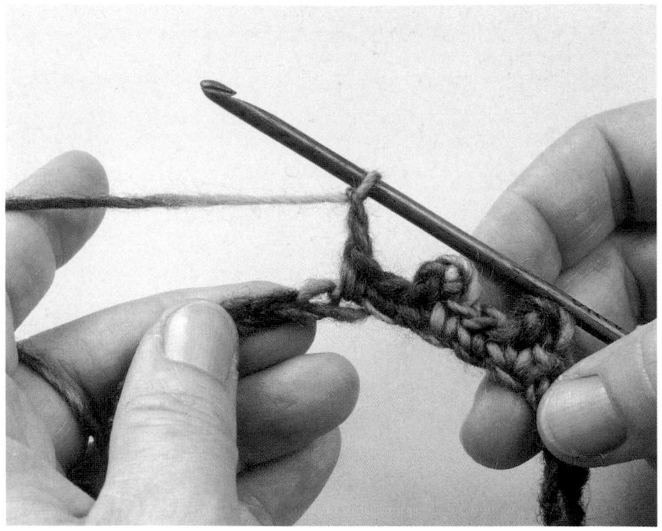

CROCHETING THE EDGING

6 Sc in 2nd ch from hk, sc in next ch, [ch 3 (see photo), sc in same ch, sc in next 2 ch] rep to end. Steam press crochet edging so that it lays flat.

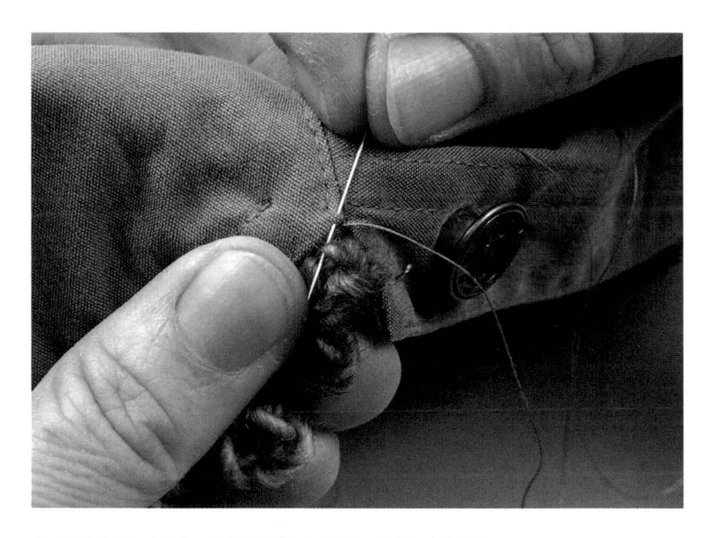

JOINING THE EDGING TO THE VEST

7 St the edging to the bottom edge of the vest until 1 inch (2.5 cm) from the end. Cut the crochet edging 2 inches (5 cm) beyond the end of the vest and unravel the sts so the last finished st lines up with the end of the vest. Weave the tails of yarn into the crochetwork and clip the tail close to the crochetwork. Finish stitching the edging to the vest. Rep for the edging on the collar of the vest, weaving in the loose tails at the beg of the edging (see photo).

Mini Belt Bag

Crochet doesn't come any faster or easier than this handsome belt bag. Use this pattern as an exercise in color exploration and to learn simple fringing. Be sure to make extras to give away as last-minute gifts.

YOU WILL NEED

1 skein beige sport weight yarn that will obtain gauge given below; approximately 1.75 ounces (50 g), or 154 yards (142 m)

1 skein black sport weight yarn; approximately 1.75 ounces (50 g), or 154 yards (142 m)

1 skein white sport weight yarn; approximately 2 ounces (50 g), or 120 yards (110 m)

Size D hook

Size E hook

Size G hook

Tapestry needle

Scissors

FINISHED MEASUREMENTS

2½ inches (6.4 cm) x 3¼ inches (8.3 cm) plus 2 inches (5 cm) fringe

GAUGE (in sc)

5 sts = 1 inch (2.5 cm)

6 rows = 1 inch (2.5 cm)

STITCHES USED

ch

sc

dc

fpdc

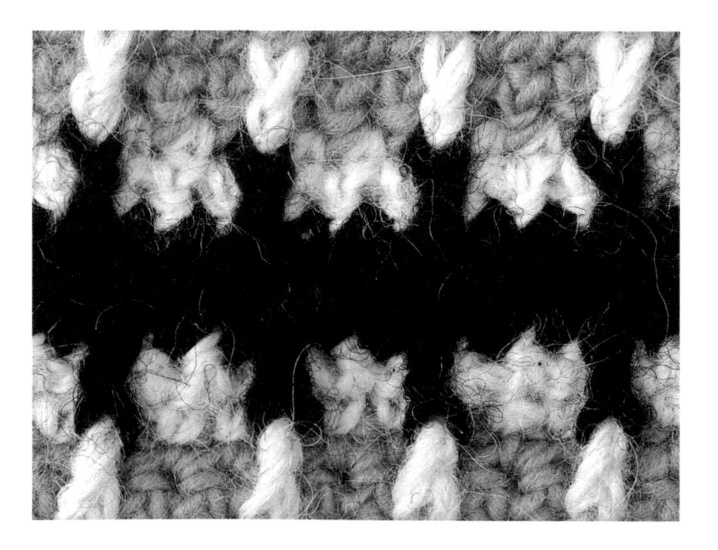

CREATING THE LEFT FRONT

1 Foundation: With the size E hk and the beige yarn, ch 16, turn.

Row 1: Ch 1, sc in 2nd ch from hk and every ch across, turn.
Rows 2–4: Ch 1, sc in every ch across.
Row 5: Change to white yarn, ch 1 [sc in next 2 sts, fpdc 2 rows below] 4 times, sc in next 4 sts, turn.
Row 6: Ch 1, sc in each st across, turn.
Row 7: Rep row 5 in black yarn, making each fpdc around the white fpdc 2 rows below (see photo). Weave in ends.

MAKING THE BACK

2 Using beige yarn sc in each st across row 1 of left front.

Rows 1–14: Ch 1, sc in each st across, turn.

STITCHING THE RIGHT FRONT

3 Row 15: Ch 1, sc in back half of each st across, turn.

Rows 16–21: Rep rows 2–7 of the left front, reversing the st order of row 5 and row 7. Do not weave in the end of the black yarn.

SEAMING THE BAG

4 Cut the tail of the black yarn on the right front to about 12 inches (30.5 cm). Thread the tail with the tapestry needle and stitch the center seam (see photo).

FRINGING

5 Cut 20 pieces of the black yarn 7 inches (17.8 cm) in length. Using the size G hk, attach the fringe to the bottom of the bag, as in step 4, page 36, of the Fern Forest Scarf, closing the bottom edges together (see photo). Cut the loose ends of the fringe even to about 2 inches (5 cm) long.

CONSTRUCTING THE BELT CASING

6 The casing must be large enough to fit your belt, so select the belt you would like to wear and measure its width. Using the beige yarn and the size D hk, sc in every st along the back of the bag on the 7th row from the top, or adjust the starting row according to your belt width as stated above (see photo). [Ch 1, sc across, turn] rep until the casing is even with the bag's top opening. Sew the casing to the back of the opening with the tapestry needle and tail yarn.

This project was crocheted with Brown Sheep's Top of the Lamb in fawn #240 (100% wool), Brown Sheep's Top of the Lamb in black (100% wool), and Blue Sky Alpacas' natural white (100% alpaca).

Fern Forest Scarf and Fern Leaf Mittens

Rich colors and captivating textures make this scarf-and-mitten set simply irresistible. Once you wrap this scarf around your neck and don these mittens, you'll know you're wearing the most luxurious crochet. Go ahead, indulge yourself.

Scarf

YOU WILL NEED

Yarn A: 1 skein bulky weight yarn; approximately 3.5 ounces (100 g), or 127 yards (115 m)

Yarn B: 1 skein bulky weight yarn that will obtain the gauge given below; approximately 3.5 ounces (100 g), or 165 yards (150 m)

Yarn C: 1 skein bulky weight cotton tape; approximately 3.5 ounces (100 g), or 187 yards (170 m)

Yarn D: 1 skein bulky weight mohair-type yarn; approximately 3.5 ounces (100 g), or 192 yards (175 m)

Yarn E: 1 skein bulky weight chenille yarn; approximately 3.5 ounces (100 g), or 110 yards (100 m)

Yarn F: 1 skein bulky weight yarn; approximately 3.5 ounces (100 g), or 103 yards (94 m)

Size K hook

Size N hook

Tapestry needle

Stitch markers

Scissors

FINISHED MEASUREMENTS

8 inches (20.3 cm) x 48 inches (122 cm), plus a 7-inch (17.8 cm) fringe at each end

GAUGE (in seed stitch using Yarn B and size K hk)

2 sts = 1 inch (2.5 cm)

3 rows = 1 inch (2.5 cm)

STITCHES USED

sc

sc backwards

dc

tip

Changing Yarns for the Fern Forest Scarf

To change yarns at the end of the row, pull the new yarn through the loop on the hk, leaving a 3-inch (7.6 cm) tail. Pull the old yarn very tightly so the new yarn is held in place. Cut the old yarn to 3 inches (7.6 cm), and continue the new row with the new yarn.

CREATING THE BODY

1 Foundation: Using the size K hk and Yarn A, ch 29, turn.

Row 1: Ch 2, sc in 3rd ch from hk, [ch 1, skip next ch, sc in next ch] rep across (15 reps total).

Row 2: Ch 2, sc in ch sp, [ch 1, sc in ch sp] rep across (15 reps total).

Continue to rep row 2 (see photo), following the color sequence below. Ch 1, sc in ch sp, or ch 1, dc in ch sp, as indicated. Make 5 reps.
2 rows sc with Yarn A.
2 rows sc with Yarn B.
2 rows sc with Yarn C.
1 row sc with Yarn D.
1 row dc with Yarn D.
1 row dc with Yarn E.
1 row sc with Yarn D.
2 rows sc with Yarn F.
1 row sc with Yarn D.
2 rows sc with Yarn C.
2 rows sc with Yarn B.
2 rows sc with Yarn D.
2 rows sc with Yarn F.
1 row dc with Yarn A.
1 row sc with Yarn E.
1 row sc with Yarn D.
1 row sc with Yarn C.

EDGING

3 Using Yarn E and the size N hk, sc backwards along the long edges of the scarf, covering the loose ends of yarn (see photo). Weave in any tails that still show.

FRINGING

4 Cut 14 pieces of Yarn A, Yarn D, and Yarn F, each 18 inches (45.7 cm) in length, and set aside. Cut 14 pieces of Yarn B, Yarn C, and Yarn E, each 18 inches (45.7 cm) in length, and set aside separately. To make the fringe, fold 3 strands of 1 color group of yarn in half and slip over the hk. Slide the hk into the 1st st on the end of the scarf, and wrap the folded strands of yarn around the hk (6 strands) as shown above. With the hk, pull the strand ends through the st and the loop on the hk, pulling the ends of the strand all the way through. Tighten the knot you just made with the strands. Rep, making fringe across both ends of the scarf and alternating the two color groups. Cut the fringe ends even to about 6 inches (15.2 cm) long.

This project was crocheted with yarns from Colinette Yarns, Ltd. Yarn A is Prism in Moss #75 (wool and cotton twist). Yarn B is Skye in Pierro #102 (100% wool). Yarn C is Wigwam in Cezanne #103. Yarn D is Mohair in Velvet Leaf #113 (78% mohair, 13% wool, 9% nylon). Yarn E is Isis in Velvet Leaf #113 (100% viscose). Yarn F is Zanziba in Velvet Leaf #113 (51% wool, 48% viscose, 1% nylon).

Mittens

YOU WILL NEED

Yarn A: 1 skein bulky weight yarn; approximately 3.5 ounces (100 g), or 165 yards (150 m)	Beige elastic, size medium
Yarn B: 1 skein bulky weight yarn that will obtain the gauge given below; approximately 3.5 ounces (100 g), or 127 yards (115 m)	Size H hook
Yarn C: 1 skein bulky weight chenille yarn; approximately 3.5 ounces (100 g), or 110 yards (100 m)	Size I hook
Yarn D: 1 skein bulky weight mohair-type yarn; approximately 3.5 ounces (100 g), or 192 yards (175 m)	Tapestry needle
	Stitch markers
	Scissors

FINISHED MEASUREMENTS

9¾ inches (24.8 cm) x 4¾ inches (12.1 cm)

GAUGE (in sc using Yarn B and size I hk)

3 sts = 1 inch (2.5 cm)

3 rows = 1 inch (2.5 cm)

STITCHES USED

ch

sc

sc in the back half of the st

MAKING THE RIBBING

1 Foundation: Using Yarn A and the size H hk, ch 9, turn.

Row 1: Ch 1, sc, in 2nd ch from hk and each ch across, turn (9 sts total).

Rows 2–32: Ch 1, sc into the back half of every st, turn (9 sts total).

Cut a 12-inch (30.5 cm) tail, thread with the tapestry needle, and pass yarn through the last loop of the crochetwork. St 1st and last row together to make a tube (see photo).

CROCHETING THE BODY OF THE MITTEN

2 Using Yarn B and the size I hk, pick up 30 sts around 1 end of the ribbing. Sc into the 1st st to begin a spiral and sc in each st around, continuing until there are 6 rnds from the ribbing, including the beg rnd.

MAKING THE THUMB-HOLE OPENING

3 Sc into 24 sts, ch 5, skip 9 sts, sc in next st.

STITCHING THE TOP HALF OF THE MITTEN

4 Continue sc in every st, making sc in each of the 5 ch when you reach them, then sc in each st until there are 10 rnds from the thumb-hole opening. Fold mitten in half so the thumb-hole is on 1 side of the mitten to the left. Mark each side with a st marker. Change to Yarn A and decrease each side every other rnd 3 times by skipping a st, then at each side for the next 2 rnds (see photo). Cut the yarn 12 inches (30.5 cm) away from the mitten. Turn the mitten inside out and thread the yarn tail through a tapestry needle. Pass the needle through the last loop. Whipstitch the seam together. Weave in end.

CREATING THE THUMB

5 Using Yarn A, pick up 14 sts around thumb-hole opening. Sc in spiral for 2 rnds. Decrease 1 st every other rnd 3 times by skipping a st, staggering decreases. Decrease every rnd until there are 4 sts left. Weave through last sts. Weave in end.

Make another mitten as above except, on the top half of the mitten, fold the mitten in half so that the thumb hole is on 1 side of the mitten to the right.

EDGING THE RIBBING

6 Using 2 strands of Yarn C, backstitch around the top and bottom of the ribbing on each mitten.

ADDING THE ELASTIC TO THE RIBBING

7 Thread the tapestry needle with a 24-inch (61 cm) length of the elastic, and tie the tail to the upper inside edge of the ribbing. St through each st, spiraling around the ribbing (see photo). Adjust the elastic as you st it, pulling the elastic so it holds the ribbing snugly on your wrist when you wear the mitten. Knot, and weave in the end of the elastic.

EMBROIDERING

8 Using 2 strands of Yarn D, ch st the stem on the back of each mitten (see photo). Add the leaves in ch st. Weave in ends.

This project was crocheted with yarns from Colinette Yarns, Ltd. Yarn A is Skye in Pierro #102 (100% wool). Yarn B is Prism in Moss #75 (wool and cotton twist yarn). Yarn C is Isis in Velvet Leaf #113 (100% viscose). Yarn D is Mohair in Velvet Leaf #113 (78% mohair, 13% wool, and 9% nylon).

Rainbow Pocket Accents

These cheerful pockets define fast and fun crochet. Brightly colored embroidery thread transforms familiar Granny Squares into stylish modern accents you can sew on almost anything. These three patterns also make excellent swatches for testing color plans and stitch motifs.

YOU WILL NEED

Embroidery threads in the colors of your choice. Each set of colors should be about ⅛ inch (3 mm) thick, the thickness of 12 strands of embroidery floss.

Size E hook

Tapestry needle

Sewing needle

Sewing thread

Scissors

FINISHED MEASUREMENTS (these will vary depending upon your thread)

Blue and Yellow Star Pocket: 2¾ inches (7 cm) in diameter

Blue Pocket with Orange Embroidery: 3¼ inches (8.3 cm) square

Bright Granny Square: 3½ inches (8.9 cm) square

GAUGE

Blue and Yellow Star Pocket

5 sts = 1 inch (2.5 cm)

5 rows = 1 inch (2.5 cm)

Blue Pocket with Orange Embroidery

10 sts = 1 inch (2.5 cm)

6 rows = 1 inch (2.5 cm)

Bright Granny Square

10 sts = 1 inch (2.5 cm)

6 rows = 1 inch (2.5 cm)

STITCHES USED

ch

sl st

sc

dc

fpdc

tip

Make a small swatch of the colors you plan to use to see if the threads are all the same size. Add a narrow thread to those that are thinner than the rest, so you won't have an uneven pocket.

BLUE AND YELLOW STAR POCKET

1 Using the yellow thread and the size E hook, ch 5 and join into a ring with a sl st.

Row 1: 10 sc in ring, place marker (10 sts).

Row 2: 2 sc in each st pulling blue thread through last st in row (20 sts).

Row 3: [1 sc with the blue thread in current st, 1 sc with the yellow thread in next 4 sts pulling the blue thread through last st's yo] 5 times (25 sts).

Row 4: [2 sc with the blue thread in the next st (see photo), 1 sc with the blue thread in the next st, 1 sc with the yellow thread in the next 3 sts pulling the blue thread through last st's yo] 5 times (30 sts).

Row 5: [2 sc with the blue thread in the next st, 1 sc with the blue thread in the next 3 sts, 1 sc with the yellow thread in the next 2 sts pulling the blue thread through last st's yo] 5 times (35 sts).

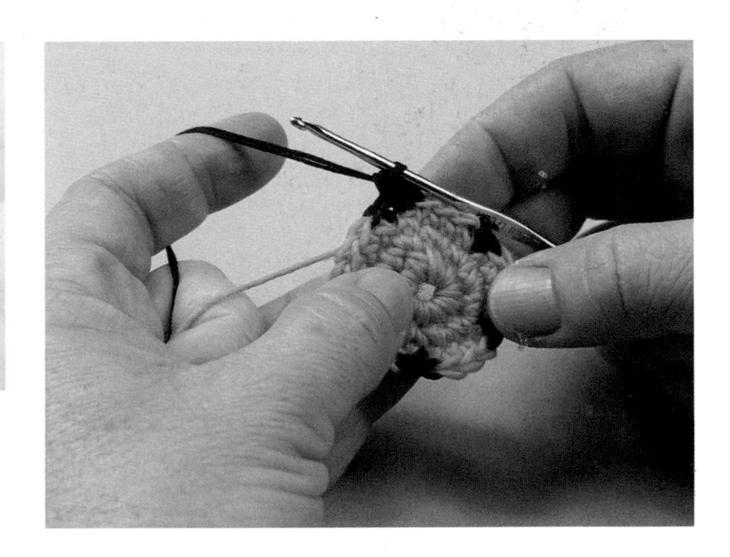

Row 6: [2 sc with the blue thread in the next st, 1 sc with the blue thread in the next 5 sts, 1 sc with the yellow thread in the next st pulling the blue thread through the last yo] 5 times (40 sts). Cut and weave in the yellow thread.

Row 7: [2 sc in next st, 1 sc in next 7 sts] 5 times, sl st in next st, weave in end.

2 St the pocket to a fanny pack or other item, leaving about a 2-inch (5 cm) opening at the top for a pocket, or st completely around the pocket to make a patch (see photo).

BLUE POCKET WITH ORANGE EMBROIDERY

1 Using 12 strands of blue thread, ch 16, turn.
Row 1: Ch 1, sc in 2nd ch from hk and every ch across, turn.
Rows 2–7: Ch 1, sc in each st across, turn.
Rows 8–11: Rep row 2 once with yellow threads, twice with purple threads, and once with green threads.
Row 12: With green threads, ch 3, dc in each st across, turn.
Row 13: Rep row 2 using a red/orange mix of threads.
Row 14: With purple threads, ch 1, [sc in next st, fpdc in green dc row] rep across, turn.
Row 15: Rep row 2 with purple threads.
Row 16: Rep row 2 with blue threads.
Weave in ends. Embroider as shown in photo with a single orange thread.

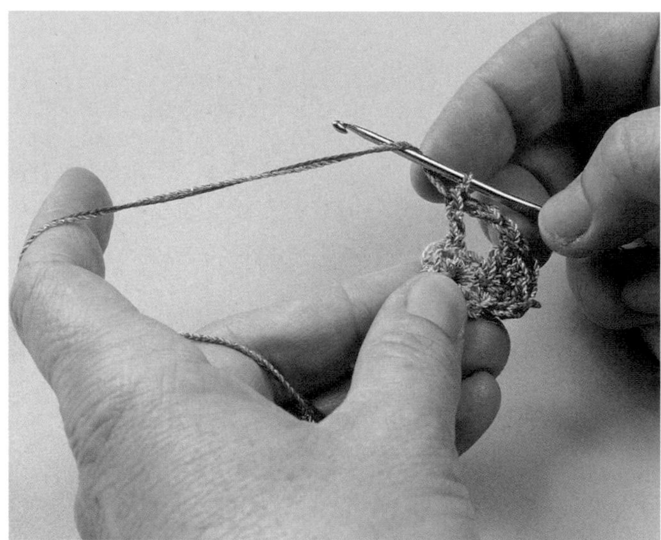

BRIGHT GRANNY SQUARE

1 With yellow thread ch 4, join into a ring with a sl st.
Row 1: Ch 1, 7 sc in ring, join to 1st st with sl st.
Row 2: Change to orange thread. Ch 3, 3 dc in 1st st, [skip next st, ch 3, 4 dc next st] 3 times, ch 3, sl st in top of ch 3 (see photo).
Row 3: Change to red/orange thread. Ch 5, [4 dc in next ch sp, ch 3, 4 dc in same ch sp, ch 2] 3 times, 4 dc in next ch sp, ch 3, 3 dc in next ch sp, sl st in 3rd ch of ch 5.
Row 4: Change to the red thread. Ch 5, [4 dc in next ch sp, ch 2, 4 dc in next ch sp, ch 3, 4 dc in same ch sp, ch 2] 3 times, 4 dc in next ch sp, ch 2, 4 dc in next ch sp, ch 3, 3 dc in same ch sp, sl st in 3rd ch of ch 5.
Continue to desired size as in row 4, changing colors for each row, and making 1 shell in each ch sp along the sides and 2 shells in each corner. On the last row, sc in each st and ch sp, making 2 sc in each corner. Weave in end.

Confetti Backpack

That special bond between you and your backpack grows even stronger when you make it yourself. Follow this easy pattern to crochet a bag that is light, durable, comfortable, and secure. You'll be the talk of the town with this adorable backpack tossed over your shoulder!

YOU WILL NEED

Yarn A: 5 skeins DK weight yarn that will obtain the gauge given below; approximately 110 yards (100 m) per skein

Yarn B: 1 skein DK weight yarn; approximately 4.4 ounces (125 g), or 256 yards (233 m)

Size H hook

Toggle closure with 1 yard (91.4 cm) drawstring cord

Backpack clasp

Tapestry needle

Scissors

Lining fabric (optional), ½ yard (45.7 cm) knit or fleece

Sewing machine (only if lining backpack)

FINISHED MEASUREMENTS

17 inches (43.2 cm) x 12 inches (30.5 cm) when laid flat with flap closed

GAUGE (in dc)

4 sts = 1 inch (2.5 cm)

2 rows = 1 inch (2.5 cm)

STITCHES USED

ch

sl st

sc

dc

STITCHING THE BOTTOM

1 Foundation: Ch 6, join into a ring with a sl st.
Row 1: Ch 3, 16 dc in ring, join to 3rd ch with a sl st.
Row 2: Ch 3, [2 dc in next st, 1 dc in next st] 8 times, join to 3rd ch with a sl st (24 sts total, plus 1 ch 3).
Row 3: Ch 3, [2 dc in next st (see photo), 1 dc in next 2 sts] 8 times, join to 3rd ch with a sl st (32 sts total, plus 1 ch 3).
Row 4: Ch 3, [2 dc in next st, 1 dc in next 3 sts] 8 times, join to 3rd ch with a sl st (40 sts total, plus 1 ch 3).
Continue in pattern, increasing until you finish the row with 2 dc in next st, 1 dc in the next 7 sts.

MAKING THE SIDES

2 Ch 3, 1 dc in every st, join to 3rd ch with a sl st. Rep above row until bag measures 17 inches (43.2 cm) from the center bottom to the current row. Weave in ends.

LINING THE BACKPACK (OPTIONAL)

3 Fold the fabric in half and lay the backpack on top. Cut the fabric the same size as the backpack, then butt the side edges together. Zigzag stitch them together with the widest setting on your sewing machine, working down 1 side to the bottom of the bag and up the other. Put the lining inside the bag and, using a narrow zigzag setting, stitch the lining to the bag along the 2nd row of dc from the edge of the bag, stitching through both the lining and the crochetwork.

ADDING THE FLAP, THE CLASP, AND THE STRAP

4 Attach Yarn B 20 sts to the left of the ch 3 on the top edge of the bag. The ch 3 will be the center back of the finished backpack.
Row 1: Ch 1, sc in each st around the top row of the bag, sl st to the ch 1, turn.

Row 2: Ch 1, sc in next 40 sts, turn.
Row 3: Ch 2, sc in 2nd ch from hk and next 40 sts, turn (41 sts total).
Rows 4–9: Ch 2, sc in 2nd ch from hk and each st, turn (an increase of 1 st each row).
Rows 10–17: Ch 1, sc in each st, turn (47 sts total each row).
Row 18: Ch 1, skip 1st st, sc in each st, turn (decrease by 1 st).
Rep row 18 until there are 5 sts left.
Work straight for 8 rows, then cut the yarn, leaving a 12-inch (30.5 cm) tail.
Attach Yarn A at the base of the flap and sc around the edge of the flap (see photo). Weave in end.

5 Thread the 12-inch (30.5 cm) tail of Yarn B with the tapestry needle. Thread the needle through the backpack clasp, and st it in place (see photo). Weave in end.

6 Using Yarn B, make a sc strap 5 sts wide x 12 rows long. Thread this strap through the other end of the clasp. Using a tapestry needle, sew the strap to the front of the bag 8½ inches (21.6 cm) up from the center bottom.

This project was crocheted with KFI's Gelato in black #207 (60% acrylic and 40% cotton) and Classic Elite's Provence in black (100% Egyptian cotton).

CREATING SHOULDER STRAPS

7 Using Yarn B, make a sc strap 6 sts wide x 48 inches (122 cm) long. Fold the strap in half, and st it to the center top of the bag (see photo), making a loop for hanging the bag on hooks or over a chair back. St each end of the strap 12 inches (30.5 cm) down from the top of the bag and 3 inches (7.6 cm) from the center back of the bag.

ATTACHING A DRAWSTRING AND A TOGGLE AT THE BACKPACK OPENING

8 Beg at the center front of the bag. At the 3rd row down of dc from the top of the bag, thread the drawstring through the row of dc, weaving in and out of every 3 dc (see photo). Thread the ends of the drawstring through the toggle closure. Tie the ends of the drawstring into a knot so they won't unravel.

Star Hat

This hat boasts toasty warmth and design charisma. Its tight weave holds in the heat on even the coldest of days, and it's a great way to practice changing colors while you crochet in a spiral round instead of stepping up in rows.

YOU WILL NEED

2 skeins blue DK weight chenille yarn that will obtain the gauge given below; approximately 1.75 ounces (50 g), or 145 yards (160 m) per skein

1 skein white DK weight chenille yarn; approximately 1.75 ounces (50 g), or 145 yards (160 m)

Size G hook

Size H hook

Stitch markers

Tapestry needle

Scissors

FINISHED MEASUREMENTS

22-inch (56 cm) circumference

GAUGE (using size H hk)

5 sts = 1 inch (2.5 cm)

5 rows = 1 inch (2.5 cm)

STITCHES USED

ch

sl st

sc

tip

As you come to a marker in your work from a previous round, remove it and use it for the current round to mark the beginning of each section.

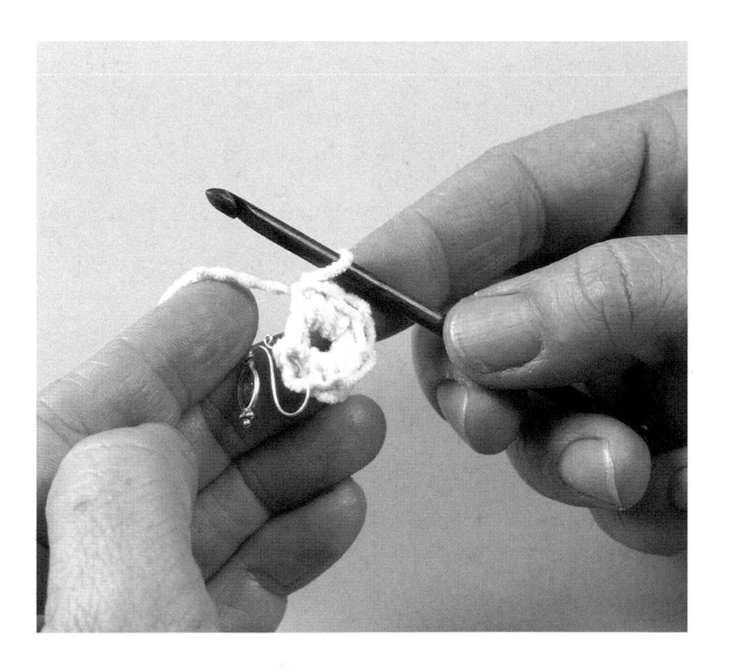

BEGINNING AT THE CENTER TOP

1 With the white yarn and the size H hk, ch 4, join with a sl st to form a ring.

Rnd 1: Ch 1, place marker, 6 sc in ring (see photo).

Rnd 2: To beg spiral: 1 sc in ch with marker, place marker, 1 sc in next st, 2 sc in each of the next 5 sts (12 sts total).

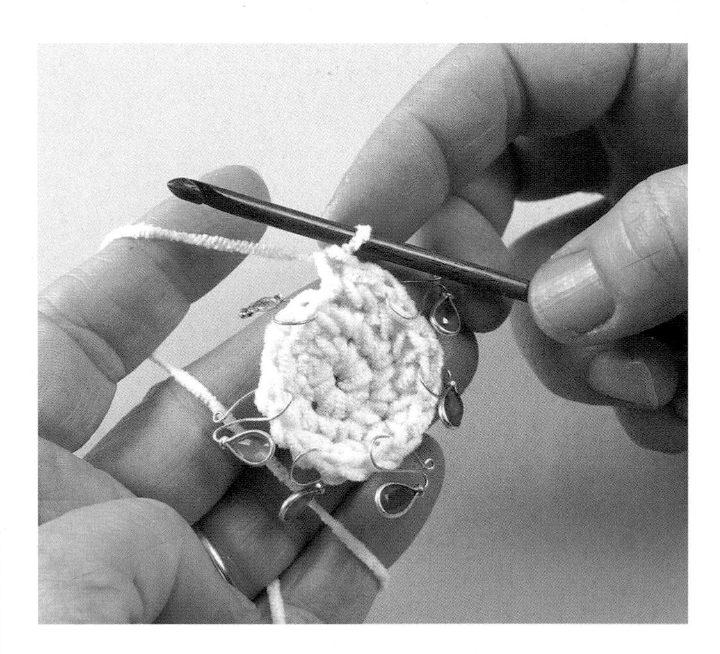

2 Rnd 3: [1 sc in next st, place marker, 2 sc in next st] 6 times (18 sts total, 6 markers) (see photo).

Rnd 4: [1 sc in next st, place marker, 1 sc in next st, 2 sc in next st] 6 times (24 sts total, 6 markers).

Rnd 5: [1 sc in next st, place marker, 1 sc in next 2 sts,

2 sc in next st] 6 times (30 sts total, 6 markers). Pull the blue yarn through the last half of the last st in the rnd as described in steps 3 and 4, Adding the Second Color.

ADDING THE SECOND COLOR

3 To add the blue yarn on the 1st st of the 6th rnd, you must finish the last st in rnd 5 with the blue yarn. To make the last stitch in rnd 5, push the hk through the last st of rnd 5, yo, and pull the white yarn through while holding the blue yarn. This is the 1st half of the st.

4 Drop the white yarn and pick up the blue yarn and yo (see photo). Pull it through the 2 loops of white yarn on the hk. This is the 2nd half of the st.

5 Make the next st (both the 1st and 2nd parts) with the blue yarn. For each blue section you will need to make the last white st end in blue yarn, while all the remaining blue sts will be blue for both parts.

This project was crocheted with Rowan's Fine Cotton Chenille in denim and white (89% cotton and 11% polyester).

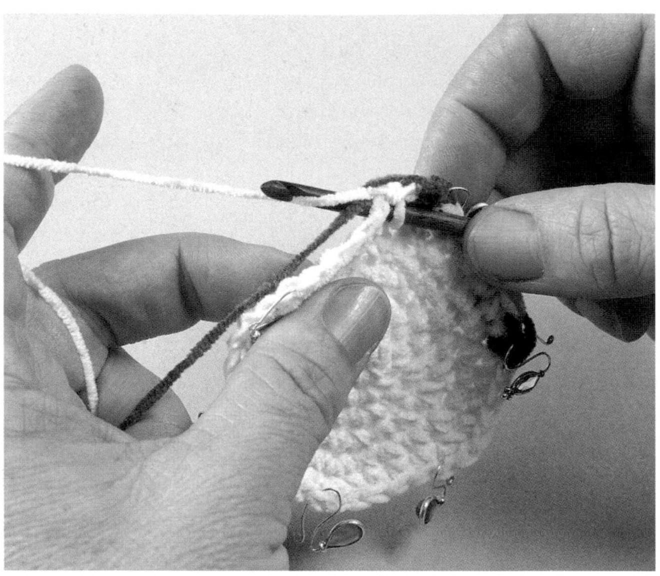

CROCHETING THE FORM

6 Rnd 6: [1 blue sc in next st, 1 white sc in next 3 sts, carrying blue yarn behind the 2nd st as shown above, 2 sc in next st] 6 times. Remove all markers (36 sts total, no markers, and 6 blue sts).

FINISHING THE HAT

7 Rep rnd 6, increasing the blue sts by 1 and decreasing the white sts by 1 in each section until there are no more white sts. Continue in blue with no increases until the hat measures 10 inches (25.4 cm) from the center to the brim. Change to a size G hk and work 2 more rnds. Weave in the end and roll up the edge until it's about ¾ inch (1.9 cm) thick, and st in place with the tapestry needle and a 24-inch (61 cm) length of blue yarn, as shown in the photo above.

Tailored Vest

The flowing colors of multicolored yarn play wonderfully off a simple seed-stitch pattern. This classic vest uses only one stitch pattern, is relatively easy to create, and will provide you with great practice in making armholes, buttonholes, and sizing garments.

YOU WILL NEED

10 skeins worsted weight yarn that will obtain the gauge given below; approximately 1.75 ounces (50 g), or 107 yards (98 m) per skein

Size G hook

Tapestry needle

5 buttons, ¾ inch (1.9 cm) diameter

Sewing needle

Sewing thread

Scissors

SIZING KEY: small (medium, large, extra large)

Instructions are for size small with larger sizes in parentheses (medium, large, extra large). If there are no parentheses, the number is for all sizes.

FINISHED MEASUREMENTS AND SIZING

Length: 22 (23, 24, 24½) inches (55.9 [58.4, 61, 62.2] cm)

Bust: 36 (38, 40, 42) inches (91.44 [96.5, 101.6, 106.7] cm)

GAUGE

7½ sts = 2½ inches (6.4 cm)

9 rows = 2 inches (5 cm)

STITCHES USED

ch

sc

ch sp

tip

When completing a row, be sure to make the last st in the ch 2 ch sp of the row before. It's a tight ch sp to push the hook through, but it will make the sides of your finished project even.

CROCHETING THE FRONT BOTTOM POINTS

1 Row 1: Ch 3, sc in 3rd ch from hk, turn.
Row 2: Ch 3, sc in 3rd ch from hk, ch 1, sc in ch sp, ch 1, sc in ch sp, turn.
Row 3: Ch 3, sc in 3rd ch from hk, [ch 1, sc in ch sp] rep in each ch sp including ch 3 loop, turn.
Rows 4–23 (4–24, 4–25, 4–26): Rep row 3.
Weave in end. Make another triangle as above but don't cut the yarn on this piece. Set both triangles aside.

CREATING THE BACK BOTTOM POINTS

2 Make 2 more triangles following the step 1 directions through row 5 (see photo). Beg row 6 on 1 of the triangles, then attach the 2nd triangle to the 1st by continuing the seed pattern across the top row of the 2nd triangle.
At the beg of the next 2 (4, 6, 8) rows, ch 4, sc in the 3rd ch from the hk, ch 1, skip the next ch, sc in the next ch, then continue in the seed pattern across the row.
At the beg of the next 6 rows, ch 9, sc in the 3rd ch from the hk [ch 1, skip the next ch, sc in the next ch] 3 times, then continue in the seed pattern across the row.

ATTACHING THE POINTS

3 Crochet in the pattern across the 2nd large triangle, then the set of small triangles, and finally the 1st large triangle you made. All the pieces are now joined.

This project was crocheted with Brown Sheep's Kaleidoscope in Phoenix #40 (80% cotton and 20% merino wool).

MAKING THE BUTTON HOLES

4 Work even for 5 rows, then make a button hole 2 sts from the right front edge. To make a button hole, work to 3 ch sps from the end of the row. Ch 2, skip the next ch sp, sc in the next ch sp (see photo), ch 1, sc in the last ch sp, turn. Continue working even, making a button hole on every 12th row until there are 5 button holes. Work even 1 more row. Mark the side seams.

FASHIONING THE RIGHT FRONT

5 Beg crocheting 5 sts from the side seam. Decrease 1 st at the beg of each of the next 8 rows by skipping the 1st ch sp and sc in the 2nd ch sp from the beg of the row (see photo).
Next, decrease 1 st at the beg of each row of the center seam of the vest, working the armhole side even, until there are 10 sts left.
Work even until the armhole measures 9 (9½, 10, 10½) inches (22.9 [24.1, 25.4, 26.7] cm).
Rep step 5 to crochet the left front.

FORMING THE CENTER BACK

6 Attach yarn 3 (4, 5, 6) sts from the right back side seam. Work in the pattern st, decreasing 1 st at the beg of each of the next 8 rows by skipping the 1st ch sp and sc in the 2nd ch sp from the beg of the row.
Work even until 9 (9½, 10, 10½) inches (22.9 [24.1, 25.4, 26.7] cm) from the base of the armhole.
Work in the pattern st for 2 rows on 10 sts of each side of the top back.

FINISHING

7 Sew the shoulder seams together using a tapestry needle and an 18-inch (45.7 cm) length of yarn (see photo).

8 Sc backwards around the neck opening, the center front, and the bottom edge of the vest (see photo). Sew the buttons to left front of the vest with a needle and thread. Be careful to line the buttons up with the button holes on the right front.

Bead-Draped Amulet Pouch

A beautiful necklace—from crochet? The secret is using thin cotton yarn to display the pattern of this handy treasure pouch to its fullest. Enjoy collecting a variety of special beads to drape across the front or hang from the bottom of your new creation.

YOU WILL NEED

1 skein fingering yarn that will obtain the gauge given below

Size D hook

Various beads of your choice

Beading needle

Beading thread

Scissors

FINISHED MEASUREMENTS

3½ inches (8.9 cm) x 4 inches (10.16 cm) with a 12-inch (30.48 cm) strap

STITCHES USED

ch

sl st

sc

hdc

dc

GAUGE

8 sts = 1½ inches (3.81 cm)

5 rows = ¾ inch (1.91 cm)

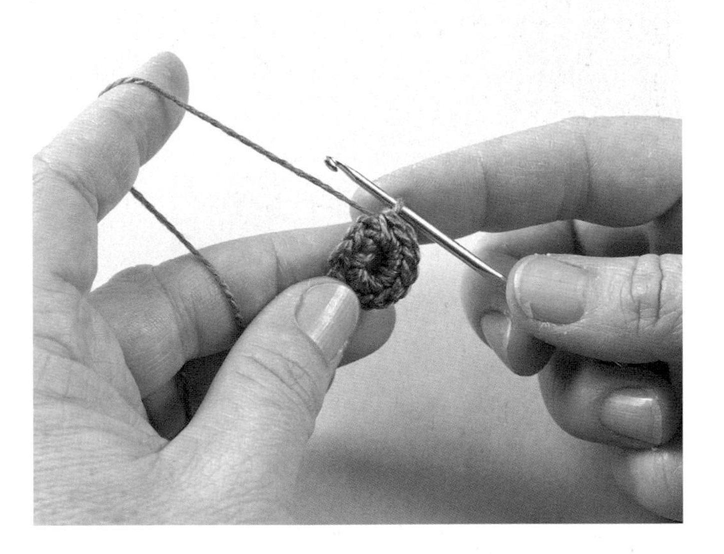

FORMING THE FRONT

1 Foundation: Ch 5, join into a ring with a sl st.
Row 1: Ch 1, 12 sc in ring (see photo), join to ch 1 with a sl st (12 sts).
Row 2: Ch 1, [sc in next st, 2 sc in next st] 6 times, join to ch 1 with a sl st (18 sts).
Row 3: Ch 1, [sc in next 2 sts, 2 sc in next st] 6 times, join to ch 1 with a sl st (24 sts).
Row 4: Ch 1, [sc in next 3 sts, 2 sc in next st] 6 times, join to ch 1 with a sl st (30 sts).
Row 5: [Skip 1 st, 7 dc in next st, skip 2 sts, sc in next st] 6 times.
Row 6: [Ch 4, sc in top of shell, ch 4, sc between shells] 6 times.
Row 7: Ch 5, [(1 dc, 1 hdc, 2 sc) in ch sp, ch 1, (2 sc, 1 hdc, 1 dc) in next ch sp, ch 2] 6 times except omit the last 1 dc and ch 2 on last rep, instead sl st into 3rd ch of ch 5. Weave in end.

STITCHING THE BACK

2 Foundation: Ch 5, join into a ring with a sl st.
Row 1: Ch 1, 12 sc in ring, join to ch 1 with a sl st (12 sts).
Row 2: Ch 1, [sc in next st, 2 sc in next st] 6 times, join to ch 1 with a sl st (18 sts).
Row 3: Ch 1, [sc in next 2 sts, 2 sc in next st] 6 times, join to ch 1 with a sl st (24 sts).
Rep row 3, increasing 6 sts each row until the back is the same size as the front.

FASHIONING THE CORD

3 Ch 3, join with sc in the back half of 1st ch, entering the st from the back.
Sc in the back half of the next st (see photo).
Rep this st until the cord is 24 inches (60 cm) long.

FINISHING

4 St the front and back together along 5 sides of the hexagon shape by crocheting backwards through both layers. St the cord to the middle of each side by the opening. Using the beading needle and thread, attach 3 strands of beads across the top of the bag (see photo) and 3 dangles of beads at the center bottom.

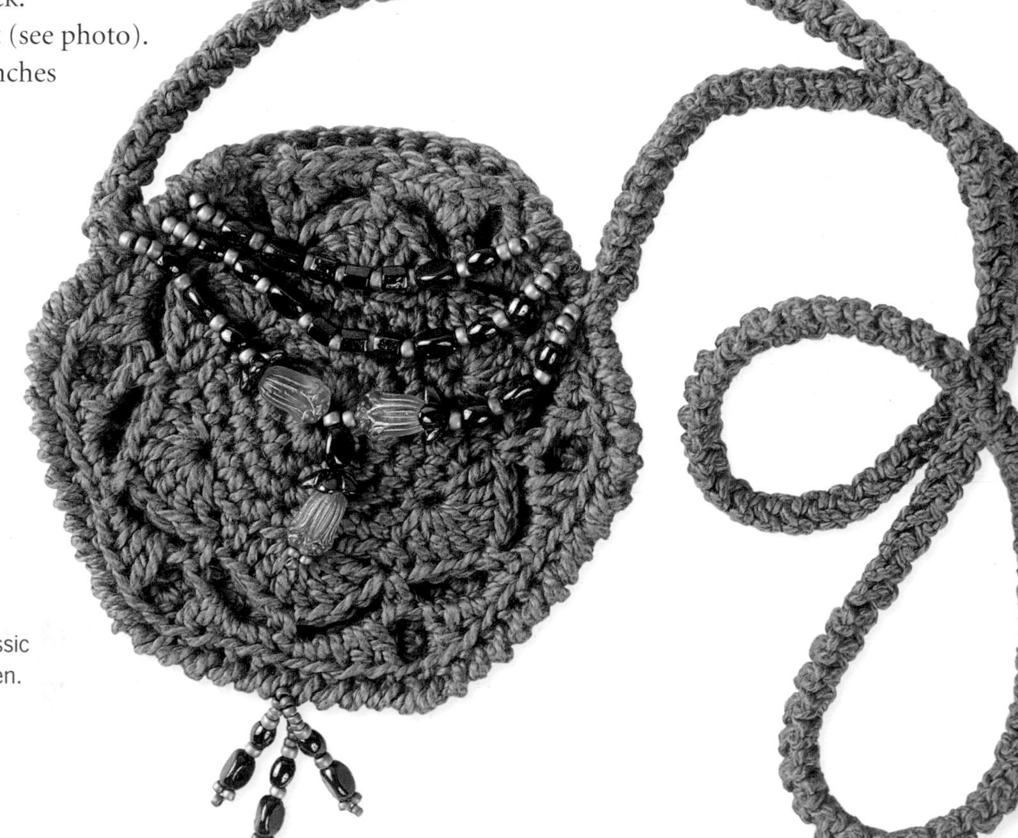

This project was crocheted with Classic Elite's 100% cotton sock yarn in green.

Linen Tank Top

Making this blouse with a fine cotton yarn flaunts its elegant stitch pattern. It's further enhanced by lace edging at the hem and picots at the neckline. Substantial yet soft, this classic tank top provides you with the perfect light layer season after season.

YOU WILL NEED

4 skeins DK weight cotton yarn that will obtain the gauge given below; approximately 4.4 ounces (125 g), or 256 yards (233 m) per skein

Size H hook

Stitch markers

Tapestry needle

Scissors

SIZING KEY: small (medium, large, extra large)

Instructions are for size small with larger sizes in parentheses (medium, large, extra large). If there are no parentheses, the number is for all sizes.

FINISHED MEASUREMENTS

Bust: 34 (36, 38, 40) inches (86.4 [91.4, 96.5, 101.6] cm)

Length: 21 inches (53.3 cm)

GAUGE (in pattern stitch)

2 reps = 1 inch (2.5 cm)

11 rows = 3 inches (7.6 cm)

STITCHES USED

ch

sl st

sc

ch sp

The most difficult part of this project is completing the edging around the neckline and armholes with the "ch 1, skip next st, sc in next st." To make a smoothly curved edging, space your sts a little farther apart at the curves than on the straight sections.

tip

To decrease at the end of the row: crochet in pattern up to the shells to decrease. Sc in 1st st of 1st shell to decrease, turn.

To decrease at the beginning of the row: omit ch 2 at the end of the previous row. Sc in the 1st st of the shell, ch 1, sc in the last st of the shell. Rep for each shell to decrease.

CROCHETING THE FRONT, BEGINNING AT THE BOTTOM

1 Foundation: Ch 99 (105, 111, 117), turn.
Row 1: Ch 2 [sc, ch 2, sc] in 3rd ch from hk. (skip 2 ch, [sc, ch 2, sc] in next ch) repeat to the last 2 ch (see photo). 32 (34, 36, 38) reps of pattern. Skip 1 ch, sc in last ch. Ch 2, turn.
Row 2: [sc, ch 2, sc] in each ch 2 sp across. At end, sc in 2nd ch of turning ch. Ch 2, turn.
Rep row 2 until piece measures 11 inches (27.9 cm) or desired length to armhole less 1¼ inches (3.2 cm) for openwork hemline.

SHAPING THE ARMHOLE AND NECKLINE

2 Continue in pattern st, decreasing as indicated. Row 1: Decrease 2 (3, 3, 4) shells at both ends of the row (see photo).
Rows 2–3: Decrease 1 shell at the beg of each row.
Row 4: Beg neck shaping, stitching 1 side of shoulder. Decrease 1 shell at the beg of the row, on the armhole side, making a total of 10 shells. Sc in next sc, turn.
Row 5: Decrease 1 shell at the end of the row (9 shells). Work even until the piece measures 7 (7½, 8, 8½) inches (17.8 [19.1, 20.3, 21.6] cm). Weave in end. Attach a new yarn at the other side of the piece and rep from row 4.

STITCHING THE BACK

3 Beginning at lower edge: Make the same piece as for the front through row 3 of step 2, Shaping the Armhole and Neckline. Work 2 rows even to raise the back neckline by 1¼ inches (3.2 cm). Finish the back following step 2, Shaping the Armhole and Neckline, beginning with row 4.

ASSEMBLING THE TANK TOP

4 St side seams and shoulders seams together using a tapestry needle (see photo).

EDGING THE NECKLINE AND ARMHOLE

5 Row 1: Attach yarn to center back of neckline and sc in st, [ch 1, skip next st, sc in next st] rep around the neckline keeping sts spaced evenly (see photo). Sl st into 1st sc.

6 Row 2: [sc in next ch sp, ch 4 (see photo), sc in same ch sp] rep around. Weave in end.
Rep row 1 for the armholes. Weave in ends.

8 Row 2: Ch 4, sc in next ch sp, [ch 4 (see photo), sc in next ch sp] rep around. When you reach the beg, sl st in ch sp and the 1st 2 chs of ch 4.

CREATING THE OPENWORK AT THE HEMLINE

7 Row 1: Attach yarn at side seam and sc in shell, [ch 4 (see photo), sc in next shell] rep around. When you reach the beg, sl st in shell and the 1st 2 chs of the 1st ch 4.

9 Row 3: Ch 3, sc in same ch sp, [ch 1, sc in next ch sp, ch 3 (see photo), sc in same ch sp] rep around. After last ch sp, ch 1, sl st in 1st ch sp. Weave in end.

This project was crocheted with Classic Elite's Provence in linen #2645 (100% mercerized Egyptian cotton).

Fair Isle Slipper Socks

Start your morning off with a smile by sliding into these lively slipper socks. When it comes to creating a cozy place for your feet, nothing beats the soft feel of alpaca. They're much easier to make than they look and can be adjusted longer or shorter according to your preference.

YOU WILL NEED

2 skeins blue sport weight yarn that will obtain the gauge given below; approximately 2 ounces (50 g), or 120 yards (110 m) per skein

2 skeins red sport weight yarn; approximately 2 ounces (50 g), or 120 yards (110 m) per skein

1 skein green sport weight yarn; approximately 2 ounces (50 g), or 120 yards (110 m)

1 skein orange sport weight yarn; approximately 2 ounces (50 g), or 120 yards (110 m)

1 skein yellow sport weight yarn; approximately 1.75 ounces (50 g), or 154 yards (142 m)

1 pair padded slipper sock bottoms, women's size 9 (UK 7–7½, European 40) (see sizing adjustments below)

Size D hook

Size E hook

Tapestry needle

Stitch markers

Scissors

SIZING TABLE

Women's Small: 5–5½ (UK 3–3½, European 36)

Women's Medium: 6–7½ (UK 4–5½, European 37–38)

Women's Large 8–10 (UK 6–8, European 39–41)

SIZING KEY: small (medium, large)

Instructions are for size small with larger sizes in parentheses (medium, large). If there are no parentheses, the number is for all sizes.

FINISHED MEASUREMENTS

Length of sole x 12 inches (30.5 cm)

GAUGE (sc with a size E hk)

10 sts = 1 inch (2.5 cm)

6 rows = 1 inch (2.5 cm)

STITCHES USED

sc

sc in the back of the st

two color sc

dc

fpdc

bpdc

PREPARING THE SOCK BOTTOM

1 Row 1: Using the size D hk and the blue yarn, beg at the back of the heel and sc in each hole of the slipper sock bottom (see photo), join to beg st.
Row 2: Change to the red yarn and the size E hk and sc in each st around. Join.
Weave in end and set sole aside.

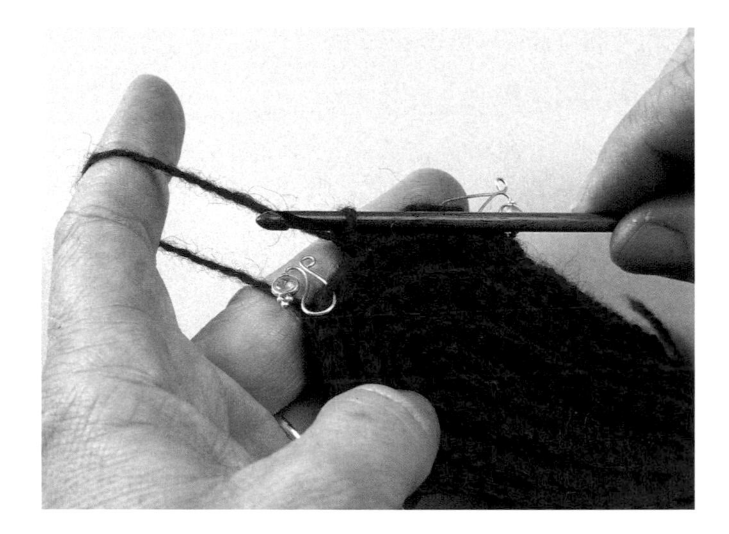

STITCHING THE FOOT

2 Foundation: Using the blue yarn and the size E hk, ch 18 (19, 20), turn.
Row 1: Ch 1, sc in back half of each ch, making 3 sc in last ch and placing a marker in those 3 sts. Continue around end of strip, with a sc in the other half of each st, turn.
Row 2: Ch 1, sc in the back half of each st to markers. 2 sc in the back half of each st with a marker, moving the marker to the 1st st in each 2 sc set. Continue along other side with sc in the back half of each st, turn.
Rows 3–9 (3–11, 3–13): Rep row 2 (see photo).

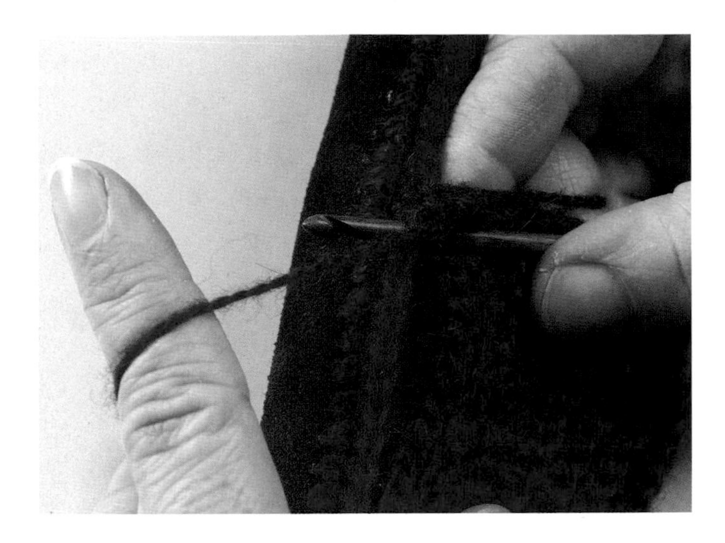

ATTACHING THE FOOT TO THE SOLE

3 Find the center top of the foot by folding the sole in half lengthwise. Mark center st with a marker. Count 33 (35, 38) sts to the right of the marked st and beg sc through both the 1st st on the right side of the foot and the red st on the sole, using the size E hk and the blue yarn (see photo). Sc through each st on the edge of the foot and the red sts along the sole until you reach the far left end of the foot.

MAKING THE HEEL RIBBING

4 Row 1: Make 1 sc in each red st along the heel until you reach the right corner of the foot (all of the red sts will be covered with sc in blue). Sl st in the edge of the foot to raise the level of the yarn for dc in the next row. Turn.
Row 2: 1 dc in each st around the heel until you reach the left corner of the foot. Sl st in the edge of the foot to raise the level of the yarn for dc in the next row. Turn.
Rows 3–6 (3–6, 3–8): [Fpdc in next 2 sts, bpdc in next 2 sts] rep around to right side of foot. Sl st in the edge of the foot to raise the level of the yarn for dc in the next row. Turn. Rep rows 4–6 (4–6, 4–8), making fpdc in the raised sts and bpdc in the recessed sts. Weave in end.

MAKING THE ANKLE RIBBING

5 Attach the blue yarn at the center back of the current row of the heel.
Row 1: Ch 3, fpdc in each raised st, bpdc in each recessed st to edge of foot. Dc an even number of sts along the remaining edge of the foot so you will have 52 (56, 60) sts around. Continue fpdc in each raised st, and bpdc in each recessed st until you reach the center back again. Sl st in 3rd ch.
Row 2: Ch 3, fpdc in each raised st, bpdc in each recessed st, continuing 2 fpdc then 2 bpdc pattern in dc along foot edge and around to beg of row. Sl st in 3rd ch.
Row 3: Ch 3, fpdc in each raised st, bpdc in each recessed st, sl st in 3rd ch.
Rep row 3 until work measures 4 inches (10.2 cm) from the red row at the slipper sock heel to the current row. Sc 1 row around. Do not cut off the blue yarn.

tip

To make the cross-stitch easy, stop before the green crochet section and complete the bottom band of cross-stitch. Stop again after each of the next 2 sections, and finish the cross-stitch for that section before finishing the sock. That way, you won't have to begin and end your cross-stitches way down inside the finished sock.

CREATING THE COLOR PATTERN

6 Rows 1–2: Attach the red yarn, and ch 1. Holding 1 color of yarn in each hand, alternate colors for 2 rows of sc, pulling the new color through the last yo of each st, and sl st in red ch at end of row (see photo). Cut and weave in the end of the blue yarn.
Sc 1 row of the red yarn, sc 3 rows of the yellow yarn, sc 1 row of the red yarn, sc 15 rows of the green yarn, sc 7 rows alternating between the yellow yarn and the

orange yarn, and sc 1 row of the blue yarn. Make 1 dc row using the blue yarn.

CROCHETING THE CUFF

7 Change to the red yarn, and dc 1 row around. Beg the ribbing pattern of 2 fpdc and 2 bpdc for each row, rep until the cuff measures 3 inches (7.6 cm) tall. Weave in ends.

CROSS-STITCHING

8 Using a tapestry needle, follow the chart below for the cross-stitch pattern (see photo). Begin at the center back and rep the pattern twice around the sock as indicated for your size.

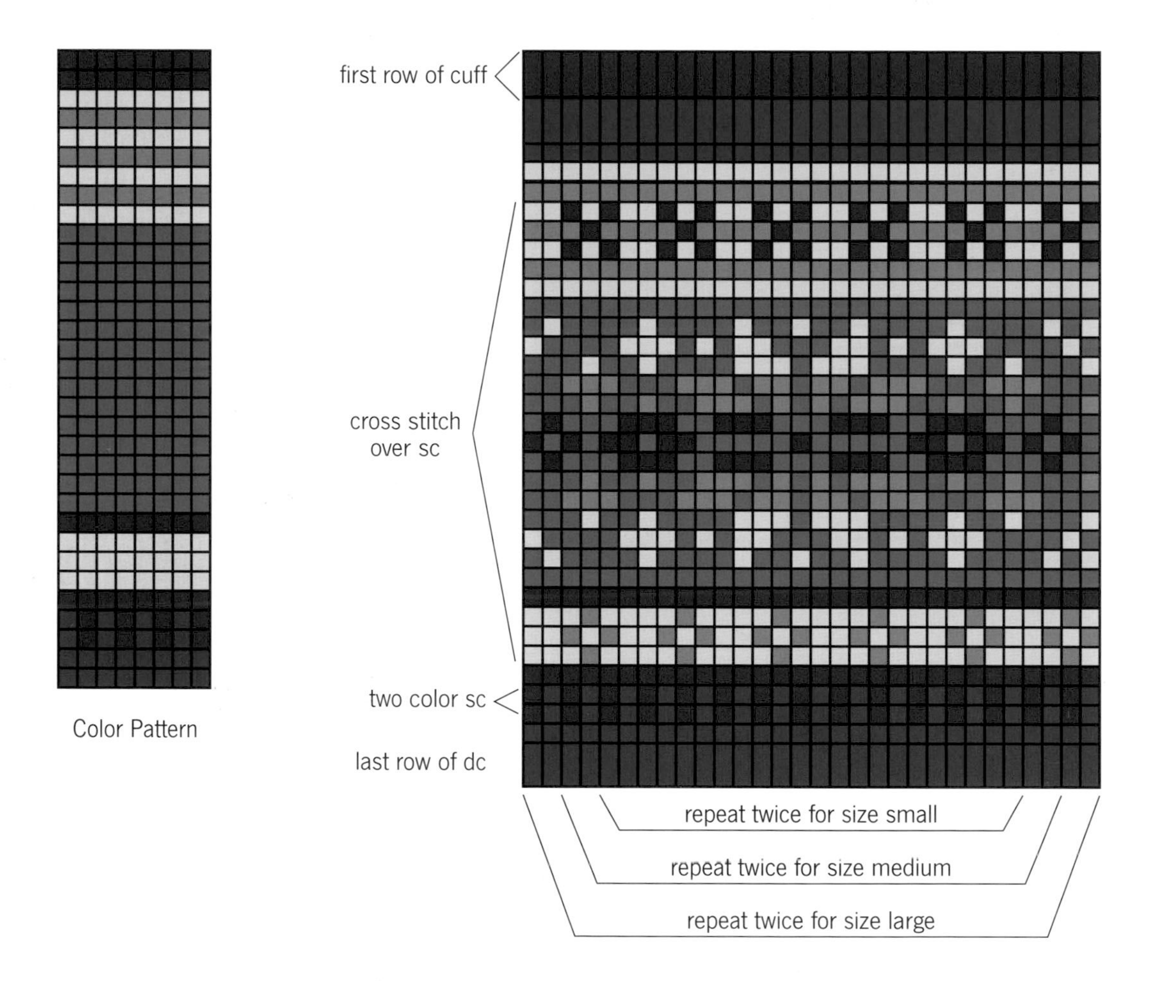

This project was crocheted with Blue Sky Alpaca in blue, red, green, and terra cotta (100% alpaca), and with Brown Sheep's Top of the Lamb Sport Weight in saffron #414 (100% wool).

V-Neck Inset

Just bought an ordinary tunic? Thinking about throwing out an old V-neck sweater? Why not give them a fresh and personalized look by adding your own crochet inset? This lovely pattern can be made in a hurry and sewn into almost anything. You'll have fun choosing just the right yarn to flatter infinite fashion projects.

YOU WILL NEED

1 skein sport weight yarn that will obtain the gauge given below; approximately 1.75 ounces (50 g), or 158 yards (145 m)

Black pearl cotton, size 8

Size G hook

Tapestry needle

V-neck tunic or sweater

Scissors

FINISHED MEASUREMENTS

Approximately 4¼ inches (10.8 cm) along each side

GAUGE (in sc)

7 sts = 2 inches (5 cm)

4 rows = 1 inch (2.5 cm)

STITCHES USED

ch

sc

dc

CREATING THE NECKLINE EDGING

1 Use the tapestry needle with 2 strands of the pearl cotton and make a ¼-inch-long (6 mm) ch st along the edge of the neckline of the tunic or sweater (see photo).

2 Use the size G hk and sc with the yarn in the ch sts along the neckline (see photo).

FORMING THE TRIANGLE INSET

3 Row 1: Ch 3, 3 dc in 3rd ch from hk, turn.
Row 2: Ch 4, skip 1st st, [dc, ch 1, dc] in next st, ch 1, dc in 3rd ch, turn.
Row 3: Ch 4, dc in ch sp, [dc, ch 1, dc] in next 2 ch sp, turn.
Row 4: Ch 1, 8 dc in center ch sp, sc in 3rd ch, turn.
Row 5: Ch 3, sc in 3rd ch on shell, ch 3, sc in center ch on shell (see photo), ch 3, sc in 2nd to last ch on shell, ch 3, sc in end, turn.
Row 6: Ch 5, sc in the 1st st after the 1st ch sp, [ch 1, sc in the next ch sp, ch 1, sc in the next st] 2 times, ch 3, dc in end, turn.

Row 7: Ch 5, dc in ch sp, [ch 1, sc in ch sp] 4 times, ch 1, dc in ch sp, ch 2, dc in same ch sp, turn.
Row 8: Ch 4, dc in ch sp, [ch 1, dc in next ch sp] 6 times, ch 1, dc in same ch sp, turn.
Row 9: Ch 2, sc in ch sp, [ch 1, sc in ch sp] 7 times, turn.
Row 10: Ch 2, [sc in ch sp, ch 3, sc in same ch sp, sc in ch sp] 4 times.
Cut the yarn to 18 inches (45.7 cm). Weave through the last loop and pull tight.

FINISHING

4 Pin the triangle in place on the tunic or sweater, making sure both ends are level. St the triangle to the row of sc using the tapestry needle threaded with the tail thread of the triangle (see photo). Weave in ends.

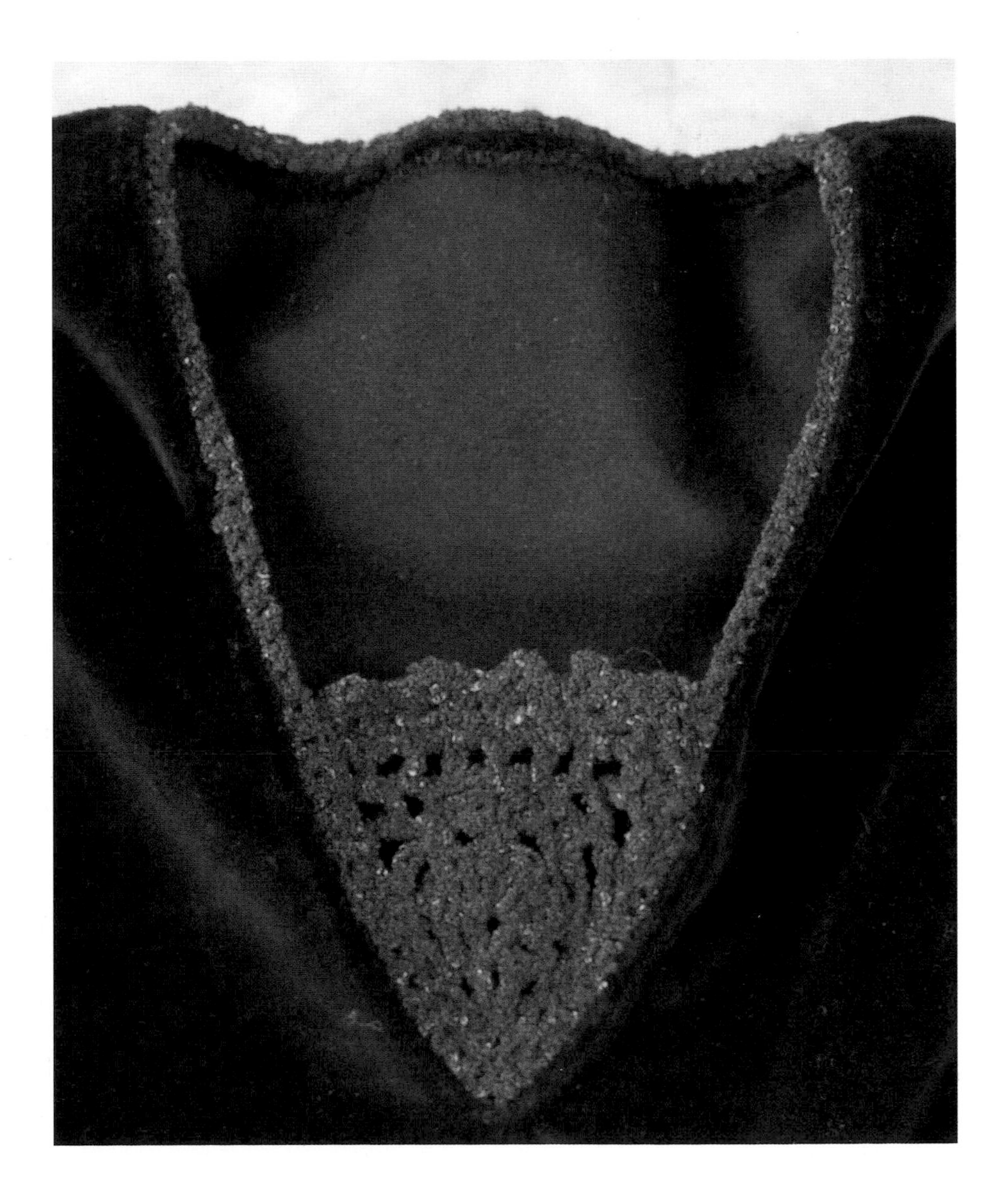

This project was crocheted with Filatura DiCrosa's Rebun in burgundy #451 (65% wool, 18% polyamide, and 17% acrylic).

Classic Cable Scarf and Hat

Frequently mistaken for knitting, this gorgeous duo has it all—extraordinarily thick ribbing, warmth, and time-honored style. It's easy to crochet chunky, strong cables. Try it yourself this weekend, to see (and feel) the sensational results.

Scarf

YOU WILL NEED

8 skeins sport weight yarn that will obtain the gauge given below; approximately 2 ounces (50 g), or 120 yards (110 m) per skein

Size I hook

Tapestry needle

Steam iron

Scissors

FINISHED MEASUREMENTS

8 inches (20.3 cm) x 45 inches (114.3 cm)

GAUGE (in ribbing)

4 sts = 1 inch (2.5 cm)

4 rows = 1 inch (2.5 cm)

STITCHES USED

ch

sc

sc in back of stitch

dc

fpdc

fphtr

tip

Every 2 skeins of yarn crocheted together as 1 makes about 11 inches (27.9 cm) of the scarf pattern. You can crochet a longer scarf by using more yarn.

Important Note:
Hold 2 strands of yarn together as 1 throughout the project.

STITCHING THE RIBBING

1 Foundation: Ch 10, turn.
Row 1: Ch 1, sc in back half of 2nd ch from hk and every ch across, turn.
Rows 2–27: Ch 1, sc in back half of every st across, turn. Do not cut yarn.

CROCHETING THE BODY OF THE SCARF

2 Row 1: Using the working yarn from the ribbing, 27 sc along 1 edge of the ribbing (see photo).

3 Row 2 and all even rows: Ch 1, sc into the back half of the 1st 3 sts, sc into each st (see photo) to the last 3 sts, sc into the back half of the last 3 sts, turn.

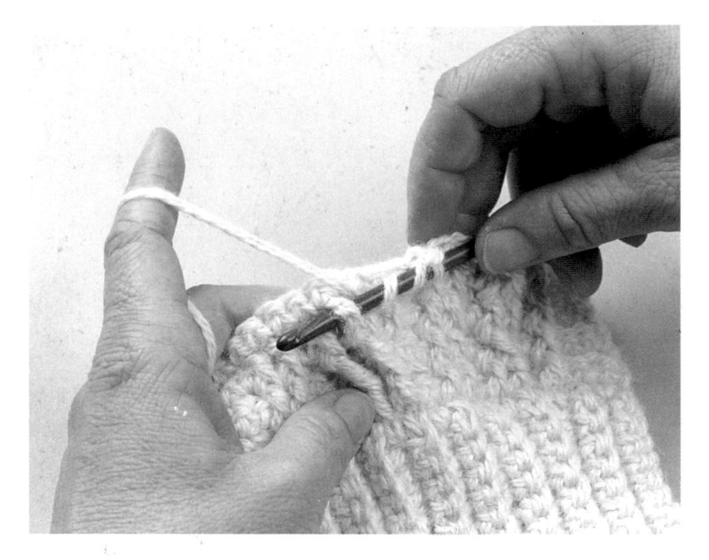

4 Row 3: Ch 1, sc into the back half of the 1st 3 sts, fpdc in the next st 2 rows below, sc in the next st, [fpdc in the next 2 sts 2 rows below, sc in the next st] 6 times. Fpdc in the next st 2 rows below, sc into the back half of the last 3 sts, turn.
Row 5: Ch1, sc into the back half of the 1st 3 sts, sc, skip the next st, fpdc in the next stm, fpdc the skipped st, sc, 2 fpdc, sc, skip the next 2 sts, fphtr in the next 2 sts (see photo), sc in the 3rd skipped st, fphtr in the 1st 2 skipped sts, sc, 2 fpdc, sc, skip the next st, fpdc in the next st, fpdc in the skipped st, sc, fpdc, sc, into the back half of the last 3 sts, turn.
Row 7: Ch1, sc into the back half of the last 3 sts, fpdc, sc [2 fpdc, sc] 6 times, fpdc, sc in the back half of the last 3 sts.
Row 9: Rep row 5.
Row 11: Rep row 7.
Row 13: Ch 1, sc in the back half of the 1st 3 sts, fpdc, sc, skip the next st, fpdc, fpdc in the skipped st, sc, [2 fpdc, sc] 4 times, sc, skip the next st, fpdc, fpdc in the skipped st, sc, fpdc, sc in back half of the last 3 sts, turn.
Row 15: Rep row 7.
Row 17: Rep row 5.

FINISHING THE SCARF

5 Rep rows 6–17 until scarf is 42 inches (106.7 cm) long or desired length less 3 inches (7.6 cm). Make ribbing as for the beg of the scarf (see step 1), and st it to the end of the scarf. Weave in ends. Steam-press the scarf to make the end ribbings as wide as the scarf.

This project was crocheted with Blue Sky Alpaca in natural white (100% alpaca).

Hat

YOU WILL NEED

4 skeins sport weight yarn that will obtain the gauge given below; approximately 2 ounces (50 g), or 120 yards (110 m) per skein

Size I hook

Tapestry needle

FINISHED MEASUREMENTS

22-inch (55.9 cm) circumference

GAUGE (in ribbing)

4 sts = 1 inch (2.5 cm)

4 rows = 1 inch (2.5 cm)

STITCHES USED

ch

sl st

sc

dc

fpdc

bpdc

Important Note:
Hold 2 strands of yarn together as 1 throughout the project.

CROCHETING THE HAT

1 Foundation: Ch 4, join into a circle with a sl st.
Row 1: Ch 1, 10 sc in ring, join to 1st sc with sl st (10 sts total).
Row 2: Ch 1, sc in 1st st, 2 sc in next 9 sts, join to 1st sc with sl st (20 sts total).
Row 3: Ch 2, 2 dc in 1st st, [1 dc in next st, 2 dc in next st as shown] 9 times, join to 3rd ch with sl st (30 sts total).

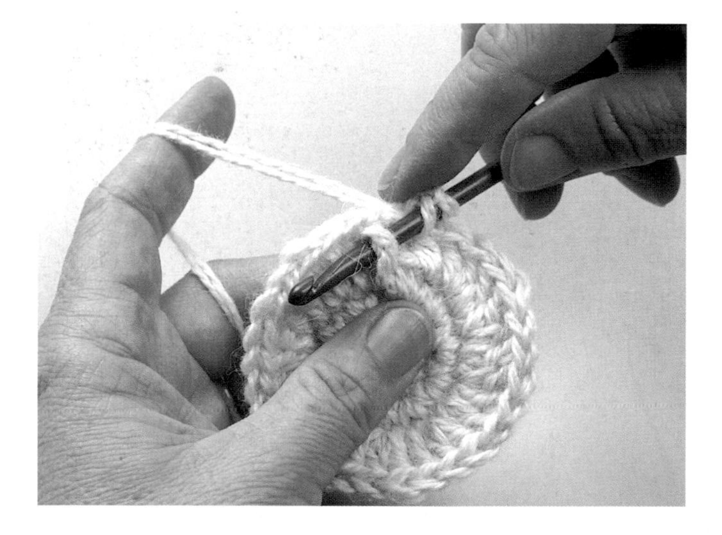

2 Row 4: Ch 3, skip the next st, fpdc in the next st (see photo), fpdc in the skipped st, dc and fpdc in the next st, [dc, fpdc, fpdc in the previous st, dc and fpdc in the next st] 9 times, join to the 3rd ch with a sl st.

Row 5: Ch 3, [fpdc in next 2 sts, dc and fpdc in next st, fpdc, dc] 10 times except on the last time omit the last dc and join to the 3rd ch at beg of row instead (60 sts total).
Row 6: Ch 3, [skip next st, fpdc in next st, fpdc in skipped st, dc, fpdc, dc, fpdc in next st, dc] 10 times except on the last time omit the last dc and join to the 3rd ch at beg of row instead (70 sts total).
Row 7: Ch 3, [fpdc in next 2 sts, dc, fpdc, dc, fpdc, dc] 10 times omitting the last dc on the last rep and joining to the 3rd ch at beg of row.
Row 8: Ch 3, [skip next st, fpdc in next st, fpdc in skipped st, dc, fpdc, dc, fpdc, dc] 10 times omitting the last dc on the last rep and joining to the 3rd ch at beg of row.
Row 9: Ch 3, fpdc in each raised st, and dc in each recessed st. Join to 3rd ch at beg of row.
Rep row 8 and row 9 until hat is 7 inches (17.8 cm) from center to brim.

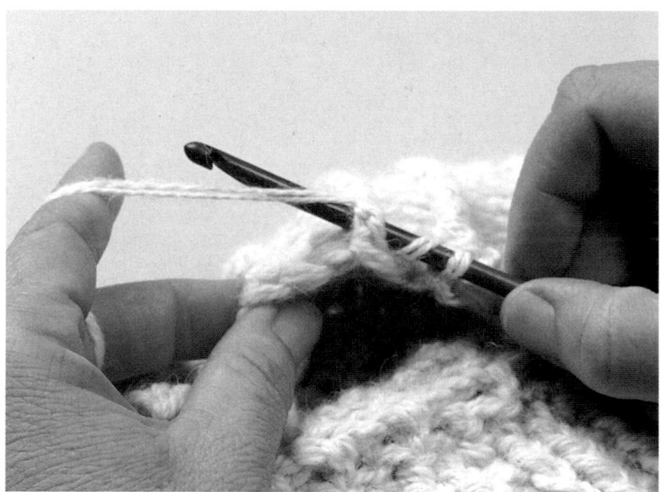

MAKING THE RIBBING

2 Change direction so that you are working from the inside of the hat.
Row 1: Ch 3, dc in each st around joining to the 3rd ch at the beg of the row.
Row 2: Ch 3, [2 fpdc, 1 bpdc as shown] rep around brim, omitting the last bpdc on the last rep and joining to the 3rd ch at the beg of row. Rep this row until ribbing measures 3 inches (7.6 cm). Weave in ends.

This project was crocheted with Blue Sky Alpaca in Natural White (100% alpaca).

Openwork Sweater Vest

Once you've created several crochet projects, you're ready for this exceptional sweater vest. Made in a hardy wool and llama blend, it's thick and toasty, yet the intermittent openwork stitching gives you plenty of breathing room. Details such as a mandarin collar and cap sleeves finish off the vest in high style.

YOU WILL NEED

8 (8, 9, 9) skeins heavy worsted weight yarn that will obtain the gauge given below; approximately 1.75 ounces (50 g), or 99 yards (91 m) per skein

Size G hook

Size H hook

Tapestry needle

6 buttons, ¾ inch (1.9 cm) diameter

Scissors

Sewing needle

Sewing thread

SIZING KEY: small (medium, large, extra large)

Instructions are for size small with larger sizes in parentheses (medium, large, extra large). If there are no parentheses, the number is for all sizes.

FINISHED MEASUREMENTS

20 inches (50.8 cm) from neck to hemline

Bust: 35 (37, 39, 41) inches (89 [94, 99, 104] cm)

GAUGE (in dc seed st using size H hk)

2 sts = 1 inch (2.5 cm)

2 rows = 1 inch (2.5 cm)

STITCHES USED

sc

dc

fpdc

bpdc

STITCHING THE RIGHT FRONT BAND WITH BUTTONHOLES

1 Foundation: Using the size G hk, ch 79, turn.
Row 1: Ch 1, sc 2nd ch from hk and in every ch, turn (79 sts).
Row 2: Ch 1, sc in every st, turn.
Row 3: Ch 1, sc in next 2 sts, [ch 2, skip next 2 sts, sc in next 9 sts as shown] 7 times, turn.
Row 4: Ch 1, sc in every st and ch across, turn.
Row 5: Ch 1, sc in every st, turn.

CROCHETING THE RIGHT FRONT BODY

2 Change to the size H hk.
Row 6: Ch 4, [dc in 2nd st, ch 1] rep across (see photo), dc in last st, turn.
Row 7: Ch 4, dc in ch sp, [ch 1, dc in next ch sp as shown] rep across, turn.
Row 8: Rep row 7.
Row 9: Rep row 7, at the end ch 1, dc again in last ch sp. This is beg increase for neckline.

Row 10: Ch 4, dc in 1st ch sp, ch 1, dc in same ch sp, [ch 1, dc in next ch sp] rep across, turn.
Row 11: Rep row 7.

ACHIEVING THE DIAMOND PATTERN

3 Row 12: Ch 2, sc in 1st dc, [ch 1, sc in ch sp] rep across, turn.
Row 13: Ch 2, sc in 1st ch sp, [ch 1, sc in next ch sp] rep across, ch 2, dc in 1st ch at end of row, ch 7, turn. This defines the top of the neckline.
Row 14: Sl st in 2nd ch from hk and next 5 ch, [ch 5, sc in 2nd ch sp as shown] rep across, turn.

4 Row 15: [Ch 5, sc in ch sp as shown] rep across, after last ch sp, ch 5, sc in center of sl st section, ch 5, sc in last st of sl st section, turn.

5 Row 16: [Ch 3, sc in ch sp as shown in upper right photo] rep across, turn.
Row 17: Ch 2, sc in 1st st of ch 3 sp, [ch 1, sc in 3rd st of ch 3 sp, ch 1, skip sc, sc in 1st st of next ch 3 sp] rep

across, ch 1, sc in 2nd ch sp, turn.
Row 18: Ch 2, sc in ch sp, [ch 1, sc in ch sp] rep across, turn.

CONTINUING THE BODY TO ARMHOLE SIDE SEAM

6 Rows 19–23 (24, 25, 26): Rep row 7.
Row 24 (25, 26, 27): Place a marker at the 26th ch sp from the bottom of the vest on the previous row. Rep row 7 to the marker, skip the next ch sp, dc in 2nd ch sp, turn.
Row 25 (26, 27, 28): Ch 3, dc in 2nd ch sp, continue across in pattern.
Row 26 (27, 28, 29): Continue in pattern to the 3rd to the last ch sp, dc in last ch sp, turn.
Row 27 (28, 29, 30): Rep row 25 (26, 27, 28).
Row 28 (29, 30, 31): Rep row 7.
Weave in ends.

MAKING THE LEFT FRONT

7 Foundation: Ch 79, turn.
Row 1: Ch 1, sc in 2nd ch from hk and every ch across, turn.
Rows 2–5: Ch 1, sc in every st, turn (79 sts each row). Weave in ends. Attach a new yarn at the beg of row 5 so both front band edges will be the same. Complete the left front, following the instructions for the right front rows 6–31. Weave in ends.

FORMING THE BACK

8 Begin at the left side of the center panel.
Foundation: Ch 95, turn.
Row 1: Ch 1, sc in 2nd st, [ch 1, skip the next st, sc in next st] rep across, turn.
Row 2: Ch 2, sc in ch sp, [ch 1, sc in ch sp] rep across, turn.

Row 3: [Ch 5, sc in 2nd ch sp] rep across, turn.
Rows 4–6: [Ch 5, sc in ch sp] rep across, turn.
Row 7: [Ch 3, sc in ch sp] rep across, turn.
Sc edging across top of diamond pattern to stabilize openwork: pick up 6 sts across the top of the diamond pattern, sl st in seed st, turn. Sc in each st across top, sc in ch 2 sp.
Row 8: Ch 2, sc in 1st ch of ch 2 sp, [ch 1, sc in 1st st of 3 ch sp, ch 1, sc in 2nd st of 3 ch sp] rep across, do not turn.
Sc edging across bottom of diamond pattern to stabilize openwork: at last ch sp on corner, ch 1, sc in 1st st of ch sp, ch 2, then pick up 6 sts across end of diamond pattern, sl st in seed st, turn, sc in each st across end, sc in ch 2 sp.
Row 9: Ch 2, sc in ch 2 sp [ch 1, sc in ch sp] rep across, turn.
Row 10: Ch 2, sc in next ch sp [ch 1, sc in next ch sp] rep across, turn.

STITCHING THE RIGHT SIDE OF THE BACK

9 Rows 11–22 (23, 24, 25): Rep row 7 of Crocheting the Right Front Body (47 spaces in each row).
Rows 23–28 (24–29, 25–30, 26–31): Rep rows 24–28 (25–29, 26–30, 27–31) of Crocheting the Right Front Body.

STITCHING THE LEFT SIDE OF BACK

10 Attach a new skein of yarn at the top of the back. Rep rows 11-28 (29, 30, 31) for Stitching the Right Side of the Back.

JOINING

11 St the front section and the back section together at the side seams and at the shoulders. Weave in ends (see photo).

CONSTRUCTING THE COLLAR RIBBING

12 Using the size G hk, pick up 76 sts evenly along neckline and front bands, turn.
Row 1: Ch 1, sc in each st, turn.
Row 2: Ch 3, dc in each st, turn.
Rows 3–5: Ch 3, bpdc in next st [fpdc in next 2 sts, bpdc in next 2 sts] rep across, turn. Weave in ends.

FASHIONING THE ARMHOLE RIBBING

13 Using the size G hk, pick up 96 sts evenly along 1 armhole opening, join into a ring with a sl st.
Row 1: Ch 3, dc in each st and join to 3rd ch with a sl st.
Rows 2–4: Ch 3, bpdc in next st, [fpdc in next 2 sts as shown, bpdc in next 2 sts] rep around, join to top of ch 3 with a sl st.
Weave in ends. Rep for the 2nd armhole opening

FINISHING

14 Use a sewing needle and thread to sew buttons to the left front band.

This project was crocheted with Classic Elite's Maya in sage green #3021 (50% wool and 50% llama).

STITCH AND PATTERN SYMBOL LIBRARY

Picture symbols are sometimes used for crochet patterns along with written instructions. These symbols help to clarify the pattern visually. The following table shows the picture symbols for the stitches in this book. Some are standard, and others are my variations.

Stitch Symbols

chain	ch
slip stitch	sl st
single crochet	sc
half double crochet	hdc
double crochet	dc
half triple crochet	htr
triple crochet	tr
single crochet in the back half of the stitch	
front post double crochet	fpdc
back post double crochet	bpdc
front post half triple crochet	fphtr

Horizontal Ribbing

Pattern Symbols

SINGLE CROCHET

This basic stitch makes an even, dense fabric.

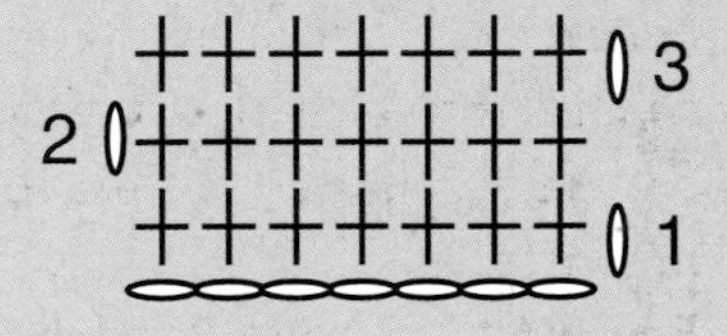

Foundation: Ch any number of sts, turn.
Row 1: Ch 1, sc in each ch across, turn.
Row 2: Ch 1, sc in each st across, turn.
Rep row 2 throughout.

DOUBLE CROCHET

The elongated stitches of double crochet make it a favorite because it achieves more surface area in less time than single crochet does.

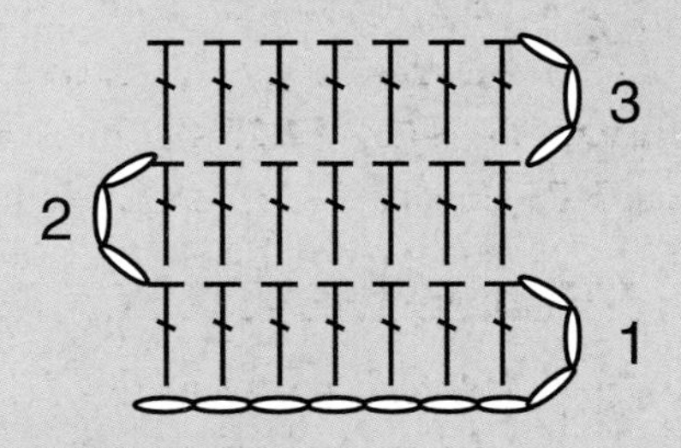

Foundation: Ch any number of sts, turn.
Row 1: Ch 3, dc in 4th ch from hk and each ch across, turn.
Row 2: Ch 3, dc in each st across, turn.
Rep row 2 throughout.

HORIZONTAL RIBBING

After crocheting this ribbing to the desired length, pick up stitches along one side and begin the body of the project, or stitch the ribbing to the end of a completed project.

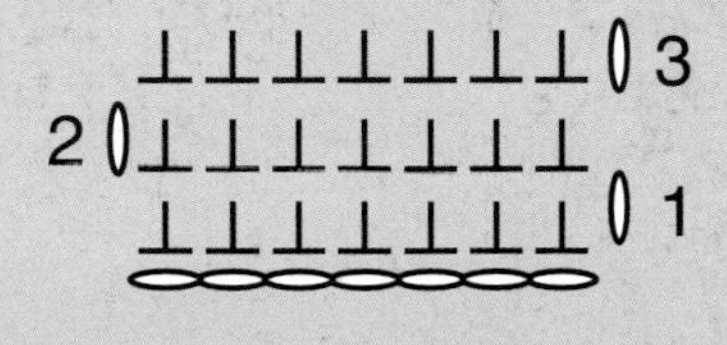

Foundation: Ch any number of sts, turn.
Row 1: Ch 1, sc in the back half of 2nd ch from hk and each ch across, turn.
Row 2: Ch 1, sc in the back half of each st across, turn.
Rep row 2 throughout.
This pattern is featured in the Classic Cable Scarf, page 67, and the Fern Leaf Mittens, page 37.

Vertical Ribbing

VERTICAL RIBBING

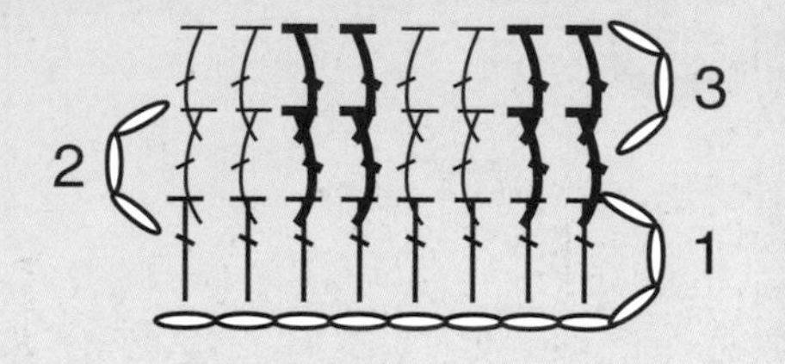

Since this ribbing progresses vertically, there is no need to pick up stitches along the sides as you would for horizontal ribbing. In vertical ribbing, the body of the project can be continued along the top row of the ribbing, or the ribbing can begin along the top row of the project.

Foundation: Ch a multiple of 4 sts, turn.
Row 1: Ch 3, dc in 4th ch from hk and each ch across, turn.
Row 2: Ch 3, [fpdc in next 2 sts, bpdc in next 2 sts] rep across, turn.
Rep row 2 throughout.
This pattern is featured in the Fair Isle Slipper Socks, page 59, the Classic Cable Hat, page 69, and on the collar of the Openwork Sweater Vest, page 71.

Seed Stitch

SEED STITCH

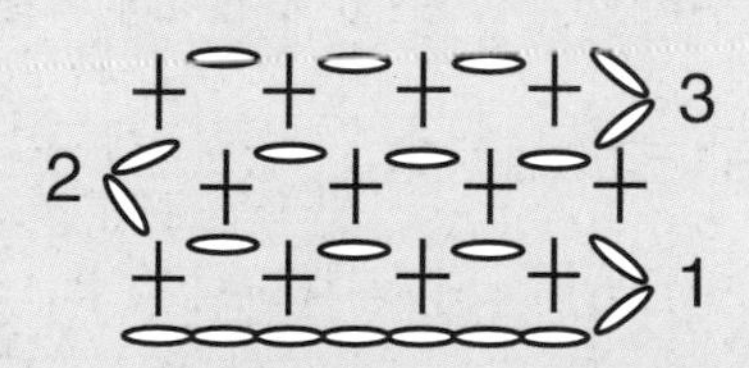

This is the perfect stitch to showcase hand-dyed, variegated yarns that have highlights of contrasting colors. Also, the stitching goes faster than many other patterns since each stitch is made into a chain space, instead of a stitch from the previous row.

Foundation: Ch a multiple of 2 sts, ch 1, turn.
Row 1: Ch 2, sc in 3rd ch from hk, [ch 1, skip next ch, sc in next ch] rep across, turn.
Row 2: Ch 2, sc in ch sp, [ch 1, sc in next ch sp] rep across, turn.
Rep row 2 throughout.
This pattern is featured in the Tailored Vest, page 49, and the Fern Forest Scarf, page 35

Pebble Stitch or Up-and-Down Stitch

PEBBLE STITCH OR UP-AND-DOWN STITCH

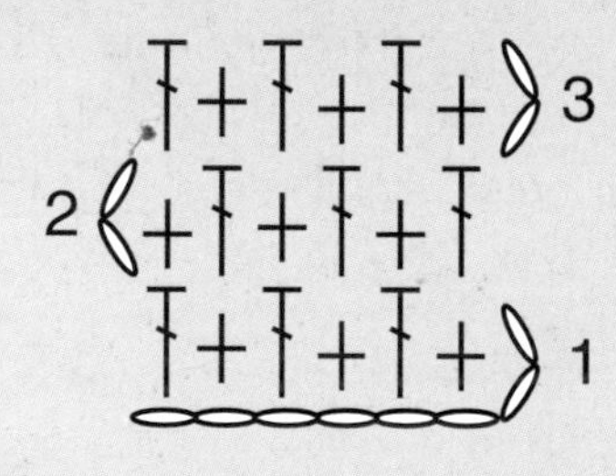

This stitch has a wonderful all-over bumpy texture which gives it a nice organic feel.

Foundation: Ch a multiple of 2 sts, turn.
Row 1: Ch 2, sc in 3rd ch from hk, dc in next ch, [sc, dc] rep across, turn.
Row 2: Ch 2, sc in each dc of the row before, and dc in each sc of the row before, turn.
Rep row 2 throughout.
This pattern is featured in the Enchanted Evening Bag, page 20.

V-Shell

V-SHELL

Here is another quick and easy stitch that makes a small open shell. It also creates subtle vertical stripes in the fabric.

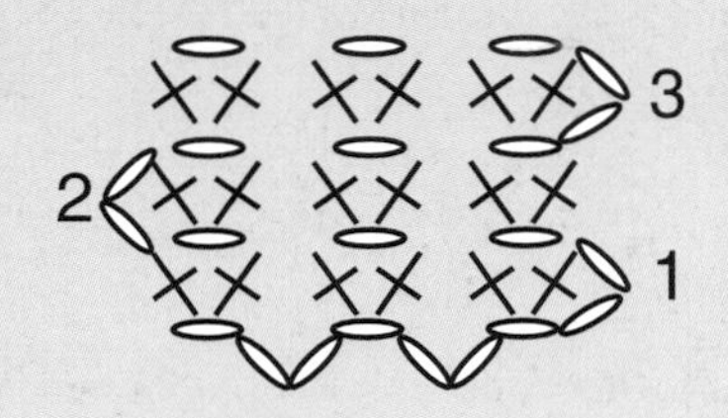

Foundation: Ch a multiple of 3, ch 1, turn.
Row 1: Ch 2, [sc, ch 1, sc] in 3rd ch from hk and every 3rd ch away, turn.
Row 2: Ch 2, [sc, ch 1, sc] in each ch sp across, turn.
Rep row 2 throughout.
This pattern is featured in the Linen Tank Top, page 55.

Open Seed Stitch or Double Crochet Openwork

OPEN SEED STITCH OR DOUBLE CROCHET OPENWORK

This great stitch is the fastest in the book. You can almost do it with your eyes closed since each double crochet is made in the big chain spaces of the previous row. As you work back and forth, the rows slant in alternating directions making a nice zigzag pattern.

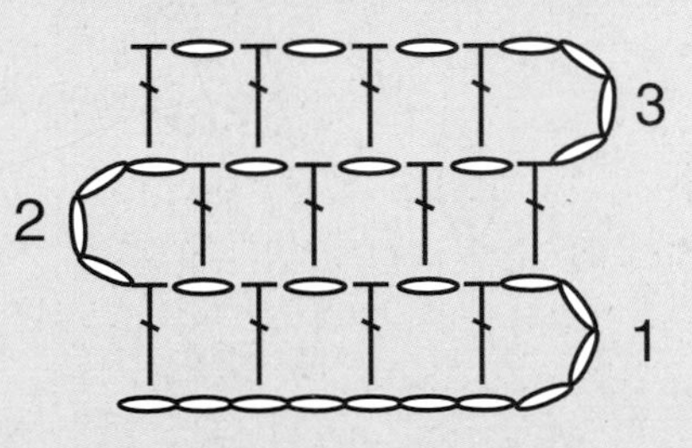

Foundation: Ch a multiple of 2, ch 1, turn.
Row 1: Ch 4, dc in 5th ch from hk, [ch 1, skip the next st, dc in next ch] rep across, turn.
Row 2: Ch 4, dc in ch sp, [ch 1, dc in next ch sp] rep across, turn.
Rep row 2 throughout.
This pattern is featured in the Openwork Sweater Vest, page 71, and the Fern Forest Scarf, page 35.

Diamond-Stitch Panel

DIAMOND STITCH PANEL

Here is an easy yet elegant inset panel. The diamond pattern is bordered by two rows of seed stitch to frame the loose chain-stitch design.

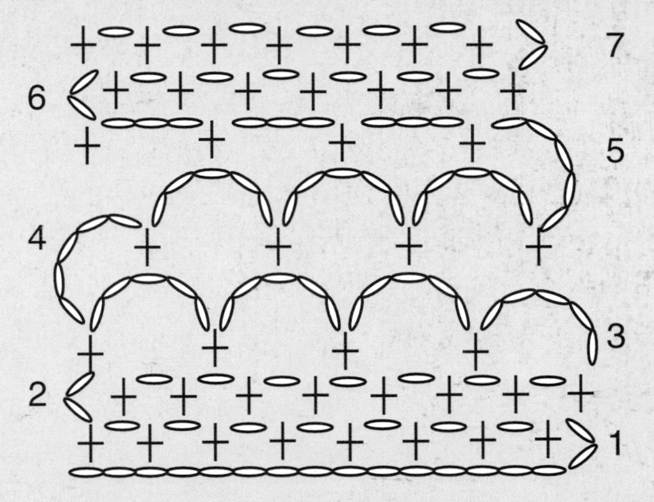

Foundation: Ch a multiple of 4, ch 3, turn.
Row 1: Ch 2, sc in 3rd ch from hk, [ch 1, skip next ch, sc in next ch] rep across, turn.
Row 2: Ch 2, sc in ch sp, [ch 1, sc in next ch sp] rep across, turn.
Row 3: [Ch 5, skip next ch sp, sc in next ch sp] rep across, turn.
Row 4: [Ch 5, sc in ch sp] rep across, turn.
Row 5: Ch 5, sc in ch sp, [ch 3, sc in ch sp] rep across, turn.
Row 6: Ch 2, sc in 1st ch of ch 3 sp, ch 1, sc in 3rd ch of ch 3 sp, [ch 1, sc in 1st ch of ch 3 sp, ch 1, sc in 3rd ch of ch 3 sp] rep across, ch 1, sc in 1st ch of ch 5 sp, turn.
Row 7: Rep row 2.
This pattern is featured in the Openwork Sweater Vest, page 71.

Acknowledgments

I would like to thank the yarn companies whose wonderful products inspired many projects in this book.

> ***Unique Kolours,*** *importer of Colinette Yarns, Ltd., carries a fabulous line of heavier-weight yarns in a variety of textures and luscious colors. Their products work up fast, and are beautiful and elegant.*
>
> ***Blue Sky Alpaca*** *makes one of the softest alpaca yarns in a great range of colors. Their thin sport weight is great by itself, doubled, or paired with other yarns.*
>
> ***Brown Sheep*** *makes Kaleidoscope, an exceptional yarn to crochet, featuring many complex color combinations, and Lamb's Pride and Top of the Lamb yarns, which are easy to work with due to their smooth texture, yet high spring.*
>
> ***Classic Elite*** *offers Provence, an elegant smooth Egyptian cotton, and Maya, a llama and wool blend available in a fantastic range of colors.*

Thank you to my editor, Marthe Le Van, who has kept me organized and on schedule, and whose suggestions have greatly added to this book.

Thank you to Deborah Morgenthal and Carol Taylor, for the opportunity to write The Weekend Crafter: Crochet.

Thank you to Josephine Shumway for the antique square button on the Enchanted Evening Bag.

Most of all, thank you to my husband, Richard, and my wonderful sons, Jeffrey, Andrew, and Jonathan. I could not have completed this book without your patience, help, and understanding.

INDEX

Mount Laurel Library
100 Walt Whitman Avenue
Mt. Laurel, NJ 08054-9539
856-234-7319